Steck-Vaughn

TABE FUNDAMENTALS

Focus on Skills

LEVEL A Reading, Language, and Spelling

Reviewers

Victor Gathers
Regional Coordinator of Adult Services
New York City Department of Education
Brooklyn Adult Learning Center
Brooklyn, New York

Brannon Lentz
Assistant Director of Adult Education/Skills
Training
Northwest Shoals Community College
Muscle Shoals, Alabama

Jean Pierre-Pipkin, Ed.D.
Director of Beaumont I.S.D. Adult Education
Cooperative Consortium
Beaumont, Texas

D1203232

STECK-VAUGHN

Harcourt Supplemental Publishers

www.steck-vaughn.com

Acknowledgments

Supervising Editor: Julie Higgins

Editor: Sharon Sargent

Associate Director of Design: Joyce Spicer

Supervising Designer: Pamela Heaney

Production Manager: Mychael Ferris

Production Coordinator: Heather Jernt

Senior Media Researcher: Alyx Kellington

Design and Composition: The Format Group, LLC

Photo Credits: P. iv ©Bluestone Productions/SuperStock Royalty Free; p. 2 ©HIRB/Index Stock Imagery; p. 4 ©Bob Daemmrich/The Image Works; p. 6 ©Spencer Grant/PhotoEdit; p. 18 Courtesy University of Chicago Library.

Illustrations: P. 14 Andrew Lankes; pp. 24, 26, 34, 40 Francine Mastrangelo; pp. 13, 22, 31, 44, 46 Bob Novak.

From *Barrio Boy* by Ernesto Galarza. Copyright © 1971 by University of Notre Dame Press. Notre Dame IN 46556. (pp. 14–15)

By Carson McCullers, from *The Member of the Wedding*, copyright © 1951 by Carson McCullers. Reprinted by permission of New Directions Publishing Corp. (p. 16)

ISBN 0-7398-8042-X

TABE® is a trademark of McGraw-Hill, Inc. Such company has neither endorsed nor authorized this publication.

Printed in the United States of America.

1 2 3 4 5 6 7 8 9 0 TPO 09 08 07 06 05 04 03

Contents

To the Learner

Congratulations on your decision to study for the TABE! You are taking an important step in your educational career. This book will help you do your best on the TABE. You'll also find hints and strategies that will help you prepare for test day. Practice these skills—your success lies in your hands.

What Is the TABE?

TABE stands for the Tests of Adult Basic Education. These paper-and-pencil tests, published by McGraw-Hill, measure your progress on basic skills. There are five tests in all: Reading, Mathematics Computation, Applied Mathematics, Language, and Spelling.

TABE Levels M, D, and A

Test	Number of Items	Suggested Working Time (in minutes)
1 Reading	50	50
2 Mathematics Computation	25	15
3 Applied Mathematics	50	50
4 Language	55	39
5 Spelling	20	10

Test 1 Reading

This test measures basic reading skills. The main concepts covered by this test are word meaning, critical thinking, and understanding basic information.

Many things on this test will look familiar to you. They include documents and forms necessary to your everyday life, such as directions, bank statements, maps, and consumer labels. The test also includes items that measure your ability to find and use information from a dictionary, table of contents, or library computer display. The TABE also tests a learner's understanding of fiction and nonfiction passages.

Test 2 Mathematics Computation

Test 2 covers adding, subtracting, multiplying, and dividing. On the test you must use these skills with whole numbers, fractions, decimals, integers, and percents.

The skills covered in the Mathematics Computation test are the same skills you use daily to balance your checkbook, double a recipe, or fix your car.

Test 3 Applied Mathematics

The Applied Mathematics test links mathematical ideas to real-world situations. Many things you do every day require basic math. Making budgets, cooking, and doing your taxes all take math. The test covers pre-algebra, algebra, and geometry, too. Adults need to use all these skills.

Some questions will relate to one theme. Auto repairs could be the subject, for example. The question could focus on the repair schedule. For example, you know when you last had your car repaired. You also know how often you have to get it repaired. You might have to predict the next maintenance date.

Many of the items will not require you to use a specific strategy or formula to get the correct answer. Instead this test challenges you to use your own problem-solving strategies to answer the question.

Test 4 Language

The Language test asks you to analyze different types of writing. Examples are business letters, resumes, job reports, and essays. For each task, you have to show you understand good writing skills.

The questions fit adult interests and concerns. Some questions ask you to think about what is wrong in the written material. In other cases, you will correct sentences and paragraphs.

Test 5 Spelling

In everyday life, you need to spell correctly, especially in the workplace. The spelling words on this test are words that many people misspell and words that are commonly used in adult writing.

Test-Taking Tips

1. Read the directions very carefully. Make sure you read through them word for word. If you are not sure what the question says, ask the person giving the test to explain it to you.

2. Read each question carefully. Make sure you know what it means and what you have to do.

3. Read all of the answers carefully, even if you think you know the answer.

4. Make sure that the reading supports your answer. Don't answer without checking the reading. Don't rely only on outside knowledge.

5. Answer all of the questions. If you can't find the right answer, rule out the answers that you know are wrong. Then try to figure out the right answer. If you still don't know, make your best guess.

6. If you can't figure out the answer, put a light mark by the question and come back to it later. Erase your marks before you finish.

7. Don't change an answer unless you are sure your first answer is wrong. Usually your first idea is the correct answer.

8. If you get nervous, stop for a while. Take a few breaths and relax. Then start working again.

How to Use *TABE Fundamentals*

Step-by-Step Instruction In Levels M and D, each lesson starts with step-by-step instruction on a skill. The instruction contains examples and then a test example with feedback. This instruction is followed by practice questions. Work all of the questions in the lesson's practice and then check your work in the Answers and Explanations in the back of the book.

The Level A books contain practice for each skill covered on the TABE. Work all of the practice questions and then check your work in the Answers and Explanations in the back of the book.

Reviews The lessons in Levels M and D are grouped by a TABE Objective. At the end of each TABE Objective, there is a Review. Use these Reviews to find out if you need to review any of the lessons before continuing.

Performance Assessment At the end of every book, there is a special section called the Performance Assessment. This section is similar to the TABE test. It has the same number and type of questions. This assessment will give you an idea of what the real test is like.

Answer Sheet At the back of the book is a practice bubble-in answer sheet. Practice bubbling in your answers. Fill in the answer sheet carefully. For each answer, mark only one numbered space on the answer sheet. Mark the space beside the number that corresponds to the question. Mark only one answer per question. On the real TABE, if you have more than one answer per question, they will be scored as incorrect. Be sure to erase any stray marks.

Strategies and Hints Pay careful attention to the TABE Strategies and Hints throughout this book. Strategies are test-taking tips that help you do better on the test. Hints give you extra information about a skill.

Setting Goals

On the following page is a form to help you set your goals. Setting goals will help you get more from your work in this book.

Section 1. Why do you want to do well on the TABE? Take some time now to set your short-term and long-term goals on page 3.

Section 2. Making a schedule is one way to set priorities. Deadlines will help you stay focused on the steps you need to take to reach your goals.

Section 3. Your goals may change over time. This is natural. After a month, for example, check the progress you've made. Do you need to add new goals or make any changes to the ones you have? Checking your progress on a regular basis helps you reach your goals.

For more information on setting goals, see Steck-Vaughn's *Start Smart Goal Setting Strategies*.

1. Set Your Goals

What is your long-term goal for using this book?

_____
_____
_____
_____

Complete these areas to identify the smaller steps to take to reach your long-term goal.

Content area	What I Know	What I Want to Learn
Reading	_____	_____
Language	_____	_____
Spelling	_____	_____
Math	_____	_____
Other	_____	_____

2. Make a Schedule

Set some deadlines for yourself.

For a 20-week planning calendar, see Steck-Vaughn's *Start Smart Planner*.

Goals	Begin Date	End Date
_____	_____	_____
_____	_____	_____
_____	_____	_____
_____	_____	_____
_____	_____	_____

3. Celebrate Your Success

Note the progress you've made. If you made changes in your goals, record them here.

_____
_____
_____
_____
_____

To the Instructor

About TABE 7 and 8

The Tests of Adult Basic Education are designed to meet the needs of adult learners in ABE programs. Written and designed to be relevant to adult learners' lives and interests, this material focuses on the life, job, academic, and problem-solving skills that the typical adult needs.

Because of the increasing importance of thinking skills in any curriculum, *TABE Fundamentals* focuses on critical thinking throughout each TABE Objective.

The TABE identifies the following thinking processes as essential to learning and achieving goals in daily life:

- ◆ Gather Information
- ◆ Organize Information
- ◆ Analyze Information
- ◆ Generate Ideas
- ◆ Synthesize Elements
- ◆ Evaluate Outcomes

Test 1 Reading

The TABE measures an adult's ability to understand home, workplace, and academic texts. The ability to construct meaning from prose and visual information is also covered through reading and analyzing diagrams, maps, charts, forms, and consumer materials.

Test 2 Mathematics Computation

This test covers whole numbers, decimals, fractions, integers, percents, and algebraic expressions. Skills are carefully targeted to the appropriate level of difficulty.

Test 3 Applied Mathematics

This test emphasizes problem-solving and critical-thinking skills, with a focus on the life-skill applications of mathematics. Estimation and pattern-recognition skills also are important on this test.

Test 4 Language

The Language test focuses on writing and effective communication. Students examine writing samples that need revision, with complete-sentence and paragraph contexts for the various items. The tests emphasize editing, proofreading, and other key skills. The context of the questions are real-life settings appropriate to adults.

Test 5 Spelling

This test focuses on the words learners most typically misspell. In this way, the test identifies the spelling skills learners most need in order to communicate effectively. Items typically present high-frequency words in short sentences.

Uses of the TABE

There are three basic uses of the TABE:

Instructional

From an instructional point of view, the TABE allows instructors to assess students' entry levels as they begin an adult program. The TABE also allows instructors to diagnose learners' strengths and weaknesses in order to determine appropriate areas to focus instruction. Finally the TABE allows instructors and institutions to monitor learners' progress.

Administrative

The TABE allows institutions to assess classes in general and measure the effectiveness of instruction and whether learners are making progress.

Governmental

The TABE provides a means of assessing a school's or program's effectiveness.

The National Reporting System (NRS) and the TABE

Adult education and literacy programs are federally funded and thus accountable to the federal government. The National Reporting System monitors adult education. Developed with the help of adult educators, the NRS sets the reporting requirements for adult education programs around the country. The information collected by the NRS is used to assess the effectiveness of adult education programs and make necessary improvements.

A key measure defined by the NRS is educational gain, which is an assessment of the improvement in learners' reading, writing, speaking, listening, and other skills during their instruction. Programs assess educational gain at every stage of instruction.

NRS Functioning Levels	Grade Levels	TABE (7–8) scaled scores
Beginning ABE Literacy	0–1.9	Reading . . . . 367 and below Total Math . . . . 313 and below Language . . . . . 391 and below
Beginning Basic Education	2–3.9	Reading . . . . 368–460 Total Math . . . . 393–490 Language 393–490
Low Intermediate Basic Education	4–5.9	Reading . . . . 461–517 Total Math . . . . 442–505 Language 491–523
High Intermediate Basic Education	6–8.9	Reading . . . . 518–566 Total Math . . . . 506–565 Language 524–559
Low Adult Secondary Education	9–10.9	Reading . . . . 567–595 Total Math . . . . 566–594 Language 560–585

According to the NRS guidelines, states select the method of assessment appropriate for their needs. States can assess educational gain either through standardized tests or through performance-based assessment. Among the standardized tests typically used under NRS guidelines is the TABE, which meets the NRS standards both for administrative procedures and for scoring.

The three main methods used by the NRS to collect data are the following:

1. **Direct program reporting,** from the moment of student enrollment
2. **Local follow-up surveys,** involving learners' employment or academic goals
3. **Data matching,** or sharing data among agencies serving the same clients so that outcomes unique to each program can be identified.

Two of the major goals of the NRS are academic achievement and workplace readiness. Educational gain is a means to reaching these goals. As learners progress through the adult education curriculum, the progress they make should help them either obtain or keep employment or obtain a diploma, whether at the secondary school level or higher. The TABE is flexible enough to meet both the academic and workplace goals set forth by the NRS.

Using *TABE Fundamentals*

Adult Basic Education Placement

From the outset, the TABE allows effective placement of learners. You can use the *TABE Fundamentals* series to support instruction of those skills where help is needed.

High School Equivalency

Placement often involves predicting learners' success on the GED, the high school equivalency exam. Each level of *TABE Fundamentals* covers Reading, Language, Spelling, Applied and Computational Math to allow learners to focus their attention where it is needed.

Assessing Progress

Each TABE skill is covered in a lesson. These lessons are grouped by TABE Objective. At the end of each TABE Objective, there is a Review. Use these Reviews to find out if the learners need to review any of the skills before continuing.

At the end of the book, there is a special section called the Performance Assessment. This section is similar to the TABE test. It has the same number and type of questions. You can use the Performance Assessment as a timed pretest or posttest with your learners, or as a more general review for the actual TABE.

Steck-Vaughn's *TABE Fundamentals* Program at a Glance

The charts on the following page provide a quick overview of the elements of Steck-Vaughn's *TABE Fundamentals* series. Use this chart to match the TABE objectives with the skill areas for each level. This chart will come in handy whenever you need to find which objectives fit the specific skill areas you need to cover.

Steck-Vaughn's *TABE Fundamentals* Program at a Glance

TABE OBJECTIVE	Level M Reading	Level M Language and Spelling	Level D Reading	Level D Language and Spelling	Level A Reading, Language, and Spelling
Reading					
Interpret Graphic Information	✦		✦		✦
Words in Context	✦		✦		✦
Recall Information	✦		✦		✦
Construct Meaning	✦		✦		✦
Evaluate/Extend Meaning	✦		✦		✦
Language					
Usage		✦		✦	✦
Sentence Formation		✦		✦	✦
Paragraph Development		✦		✦	✦
Punctuation and Capitalization		✦		✦	✦
Writing Convention		✦		✦	✦
Spelling					
Vowel		✦		✦	✦
Consonant		✦		✦	✦
Structural Unit		✦		✦	✦

TABE OBJECTIVE	Level M Math Computation	Level M Applied Math	Level D Math Computation	Level D Applied Math	Level A Computational and Applied Math
Mathematics Computation					
Addition of Whole Numbers	✦				
Subtraction of Whole Numbers	✦				
Multiplication of Whole Numbers	✦		✦		
Division of Whole Numbers	✦		✦		
Decimals	✦		✦		✦
Fractions	✦		✦		✦
Integers			✦		✦
Percents			✦		✦
Algebraic Operations					✦
Applied Mathematics					
Numeration		✦		✦	
Number Theory		✦		✦	
Data Interpretation		✦		✦	
Pre-Algebra and Algebra		✦		✦	
Measurement		✦		✦	
Geometry		✦		✦	
Computation in Context		✦		✦	
Estimation		✦		✦	

Practice 1 | Interpret Graphic Information

Numbers 1 through 4 are about using reference sources. Answer the questions by circling the letter of the best answer.

1 Which source would help you find a magazine article about preparing for a job interview?

A *Books in Print*

B *Webster's Dictionary*

C *The World Book Encyclopedia*

D *The Reader's Guide to Periodical Literature*

2 How are fiction books shelved in most libraries?

F numerically, by call number

G numerically, by date of publication

H alphabetically, by the author's last name

J alphabetically, by book title

3 Which of these would you be most likely to find in a world almanac?

A synonyms for the word *difficult*

B facts about the last presidential election

C a detailed map of the Rocky Mountains

D an article on the customs of ancient Greece

4 A reference book that lists synonyms for words is called _____.

F an atlas

G a thesaurus

H a dictionary

J an appendix

Study the library catalog card. Then answer numbers 5 and 6 by circling the letter of the best answer.

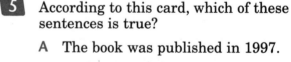

LOW-MAINTENANCE GARDENING

635 C556   **Christopher, Thomas**

The 20-Minute Gardener / Thomas Christopher.

—New York: Random House, 1997. 228 p. : ill.; 25 cm.

Includes bibliographical references and indexes.

1. Gardening. 2. Low-maintenance gardening.

3. Organic gardening. I. Christopher, Thomas. II. Title.

5 According to this card, which of these sentences is true?

A The book was published in 1997.

B *Organic Gardening* is the book's title.

C The book has 228 illustrations.

D The author's name is Christopher Thomas.

6 The numeral 635 refers to the classification of

F books about plants

G books about gardening

H books about home maintenance

J books about 20-minute gardening

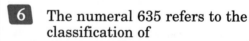

This is part of a Request for Review of a Medicare Claim form. Read the paragraph about Roberto Moran and study the section of the form shown below. Then answer numbers 7 through 10 by circling the letter of the best answer.

Roberto Moran is 67 years old. He is covered by Medicare health insurance. He slipped and sprained his left ankle while jogging. He went to the doctor to get his ankle treated, and Medicare paid for the doctor's visit. However, when Roberto went to a physical therapist, Medicare denied his claim, saying it was not medically necessary. Roberto decided to ask Medicare to review the denied claim. He had additional evidence to submit: a letter from his doctor saying that he needed the physical therapy. To do this, he used the form below.

REQUEST FOR REVIEW OF PART B MEDICARE CLAIM
Medical Insurance Benefits – Social Security Act

NOTICE – Anyone who misrepresents or falsifies essential information requested by this form may upon conviction be subject to fine and imprisonment under Federal Law.

1. Carrier's Name and Address	2. Name of Patient
	3. Health Insurance Claim Number

4. I do not agree with the determination you made on my claim as described on my Explanation of Medicare Benefits dated:

5. MY REASONS ARE: (Attach a copy of the Explanation of Medicare Benefits, or describe the service, date of service, and physician's name. NOTE: If the date on the Explanation of Medicare Benefits mentioned in Item 4 is more than six months ago, include your reason for not making this request earlier.)

6. Describe illness or injury:

7. ☐ I have additional evidence to submit. (Attach such evidence to this form.)
   ☐ I do not have additional evidence.

---

7 Which piece of information is NOT required on the form?

A the name of the patient

B the date of the illness or injury

C the carrier's name and address

D the health insurance claim number

8 Roberto's Health Insurance Claim Number is 7958305. In which box should he indicate this?

F Box 1

G Box 2

H Box 3

J Box 4

9 Based on the facts of the accident, what should Roberto write under "Describe illness or injury"?

A I sprained my ankle.

B I sprained my left ankle while jogging.

C This is a request to review a denied claim.

D The physical therapy was medically necessary.

10 Which of the following options should Roberto check in Box 7?

F I do not have additional evidence.

G Attach such evidence to this form.

H I have additional evidence to submit.

I Please find attached a letter from my doctor.

Check your answers on page 65.

This passage is about developing a heart-healthy lifestyle. Read the passage. Then answer the questions by circling the letter of the best answer.

Cardiovascular disease, which afflicts over 60 million Americans, affects the heart and blood-circulation system. Heart attack, stroke, high blood pressure, and hardening of the arteries are all examples of this disease. They also account for almost 40 percent of all deaths, making heart disease the number one killer in the United States. The good news is that you can take steps to lower your risk of developing heart disease.

Heart disease has been linked to a lack of physical activity. According to surveys, more than a quarter of all Americans lead a sedentary lifestyle. They are not active at all. Even low-to-moderately intense activities, like walking, can help. More vigorous activities, such as brisk walking or bicycling, are even better.

Eating healthy foods is a great way to reduce your risk of heart attacks. Risk factors for heart attack include (1) high levels of cholesterol, a fatty substance in the blood that can clog arteries, (2) high blood pressure, and (3) being overweight. You can fend off these risks by adding certain foods to your daily diet.

Fruits and vegetables (at least five servings per day) head the list. Many plant foods contain antioxidants. These substances prevent a chemical reaction in the body called oxidation, which can have harmful effects. Oxidation produces compounds called "free radicals." If these substances become too numerous, they can damage cells in ways that may lead to heart disease. Scientists believe that the antioxidants in plant foods help to protect the body. Antioxidant rich foods include oranges, green leafy vegetables, potatoes, carrots, sweet potatoes, and cantaloupe.

Other foods keep the cardiovascular system healthy by helping to prevent clots from forming in the bloodstream. When blood cells become too sticky, they can block the flow of blood to the heart, causing a heart attack, or to the brain, causing a stroke. Fish oils have an anti-clotting effect.

Avoiding harmful foods is also important. These include foods high in "saturated fats" and cholesterol, such as ice cream, French fries, and bacon. Use olive or canola oil, and emphasize foods that are naturally low in saturated fats, such as fruits, vegetables, and lean meats.

Finally, maintaining a healthy body weight is another key to keeping your heart healthy. In addition to exercising regularly, you should balance your level of activity with the number of calories you eat. Make sure that the calories you consume come from nutritious foods. So limit your intake of high-sugar foods such as soft drinks and candy.

1 The second paragraph states that "more than a quarter of all Americans lead a *sedentary* lifestyle." Which of these words has the <u>opposite</u> meaning of the word *sedentary?*

A lazy

B active

C unhealthy

D thoughtful

2 According to the passage, *"vigorous* activities" are good for your heart. Which of these words has the <u>same</u> meaning as the word *vigorous?*

F difficult

G energetic

H moderate

J dangerous

3 The passage states that some foods help to "prevent *clots* from forming in the bloodstream." Which of these words has the <u>same</u> meaning as the word *clots?*

A cells

B spaces

C networks

D blockages

4 According to the passage, "oxidation produces *compounds* called 'free radicals.'" Which of these words has the <u>same</u> meaning as the word *compounds?*

F gases

G camps

H liquids

J substances

5 The third paragraph of the passage says, "You can *fend off* these risks by adding certain foods to your daily diet." Which of these has the <u>same</u> meaning as *fend off?*

A accept

B increase

C eliminate

D guard against

6 The last paragraph of the passage says that the calories you consume should "come from *nutritious* foods." Which of these words has the <u>opposite</u> meaning of the word *nutritious?*

F tasty

G unhealthy

H uncooked

J low-calorie

Check your answers on page 65.

This passage is about fighting forest fires. Read the passage. Then answer the questions by circling the letter of the best answer.

Wildfires burn several million acres of forest in the United States each year. Most of these unplanned and uncontrolled fires are caused by human carelessness. One in five is the result of failing to control a campfire. One in ten is caused by a careless smoker. Far fewer forest fires are caused by lightning. Weather conditions such as extreme drought and low humidity also make an area more susceptible to fires.

Foresters constantly survey the forest to try to spot fires before they can spread. Most of this surveillance is done by airplane or helicopter. When a fire is detected, forest patrols determine how fast it is moving. Then they map the fire's location on a detailed map of the area and develop a strategy for controlling the blaze. On the ground, firefighters use two-way radios to stay in touch with each other and the command center, which may be located in a helicopter overhead. In turn, the control center monitors weather conditions and wind direction to help direct the battle against the fire.

The basic technique for fighting forest fires is the firebreak—a strip of land in front of the moving fire that is cleared of flammable material such as leaves, trees, and shrubs. Firefighters use shovels, chainsaws, rakes, hoes, and leaf blowers to clear areas and dig furrows that will halt the fire. Where possible, helicopters bring in bulldozers and plows. Where resources permit, airplanes and helicopters may also drop water "bombs" or chemicals on the sides of the fire break clearing to slow down an advancing fire.

Firefighting is a very risky job because winds are hard to predict, and a sudden change in wind direction can quickly change the path of the fire. Winds also help the fire spread rapidly. Flames can leap from treetop to treetop across a firebreak, putting the firefighters below in great danger.

The biggest challenge in fighting a forest fire is getting the people and equipment to the right place at the right time. Good communication and coordination are critical, not only for stopping the fire, but also for ensuring the safety of the firefighters.

1 Which of these tools is used to fight most forest fires?

A   lasers

B   shovels

C   bulldozers

D   water hoses

2 Which of these events happens last in fighting a forest fire?

F   A firebreak is built.

G   A fire is spotted from the air.

H   A fire's direction is determined.

J   A strategy is developed for fighting the fire.

3 According to the passage, which of these factors makes firefighting especially risky?

A   neglected campfires

B   traveling by helicopter

C   changes in wind direction

D   hiking long distances over rough terrain

4 How are most forest fires spotted?

F   by satellite

G   by planes and helicopters

H   by campers and backpackers

J   by foresters in lookout towers

5 Which best describes the cause of most forest fires?

A   drought

B   humans

C   smokers

D   lightning

6 According to the passage, which factor is especially critical to success in fighting a forest fire?

F   plenty of wind

G   plenty of water

H   a "can-do" attitude

J   good communication

Check your answers on pages 65–66.

Practice 4 Construct Meaning

This excerpt is from *Barrio Boy*, an autobiography by Ernesto Galarza. Galarza was born in Mexico, but he was raised in Arizona and California. While living in Sacramento, California, Galarza went to Lincoln School, a melting pot of immigrant children and "home-grown Americans." His first grade teacher was Miss Ryan and the school principal was Miss Nettie Hopley. Read the excerpt. Then answer the questions by circling the letter of the best answer.

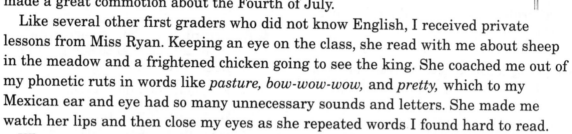

America was all around us, in and out of the barrio. Abruptly we had to forget the ways of shopping in a *mercado* and learn those of shopping in a corner grocery store or department store. The Americans paid no attention to the Fifth of May, but they made a great commotion about the Fourth of July.

Like several other first graders who did not know English, I received private lessons from Miss Ryan. Keeping an eye on the class, she read with me about sheep in the meadow and a frightened chicken going to see the king. She coached me out of my phonetic ruts in words like *pasture, bow-wow-wow,* and *pretty,* which to my Mexican ear and eye had so many unnecessary sounds and letters. She made me watch her lips and then close my eyes as she repeated words I found hard to read.

When we came to know each other better, I tried interrupting to tell Miss Ryan how we said it in Spanish. It didn't work. She only said "oh" and went on with *pasture, bow-wow-wow,* and *pretty*. It was as if in that closet we were both discovering together the secrets of the English language and grieving together over the tragedies of Bo-Peep. The main reason that I was graduated with honors from the first grade was that I had fallen in love with Miss Ryan. Her radiant, no-nonsense character made us either afraid not to love her or love her so we would not be afraid. I am not sure which. It was not only that we sensed she was with it, but also that she was with us.

Like the first grade, the rest of Lincoln School was a sampling of the lower part of town where many races made their home. My pals in the second grade were Kazushi, whose parents spoke only Japanese, Matti, a skinny Italian boy, and Manual, a fat Portuguese who would never get into a fight, but wrestled you to the ground and just sat on you. Our assortment of nationalities included Koreans, Yugoslavs, Poles, Irish, and home-grown Americans.

Miss Hopley and her teachers never let us forget why we were at Lincoln: for those who were alien, to become good Americans; for those who were so born, to accept the rest of us. Off the school grounds we traded the same insults we heard from our elders. On the playground we were sure to be marched up to the principal's office for calling someone an insulting name. The school was not so much a melting pot as a griddle where Miss Hopley and her helpers warmed knowledge into us and roasted racial hatreds out of us.

The lower part of town was a collage of nationalities in the middle of which Miss Nettie Hopley kept school with discipline and compassion.

In the years we lived in the lower part of town, La Leen-Con, as my family called it, became a benchmark in our lives.

Reading, Language, and Spelling

1 According to the passage, using racial insults on the playground would lead to

A private English lessons

B a visit to Miss Ryan's class

C a wrestling match with Manual

D a visit to the principal's office

2 Which of these statements from the passage best states the main idea?

F Miss Hopley and her teachers never let us forget why we were at Lincoln: for those who were alien, to become good Americans; for those who were so born, to accept the rest of us.

G The school was not so much a melting pot as a griddle where Miss Hopley and her helpers warmed knowledge into us and roasted racial hatreds out of us.

H The main reason that I was graduated with honors from the first grade was that I had fallen in love with Miss Ryan.

J In the years we lived in the lower part of town, La Leen-Con, as my family called it, became a benchmark in our lives.

3 According to the passage, what kind of student is Ernesto?

A a slow learner who is easily bored

B a competitive student who excels at everything

C a motivated student who wants to please his family

D a sensitive student who graduated from first grade with honors

4 What evidence shows that living in a multicultural neighborhood promoted racial tolerance?

F Racial tolerance was enforced by the principal.

G Racial insults were only tolerated off school grounds.

H Ernesto had friends of many different nationalities.

J The school and the town were a collage of nationalities.

5 The passage suggests that Ernesto's learning English was most influenced by

A Miss Hopley

B his classmates

C Miss Ryan

D his family

6 According to the passage, what is most likely true about Miss Ryan?

F She is a great lip reader.

G She is a kind and patient teacher.

H She falls in love with all of her students.

J She wanted to become the school principal.

Check your answers on page 66.

Here are three excerpts from *The Member of the Wedding*, a play by Carson McCullers set in a southern town in the 1940s. Frankie is a motherless young girl who has just learned that her brother Jarvis is getting married. Frankie's companions are Berenice, the family cook, and John Henry, her little cousin. Read the excerpts. Then answer the questions by circling the letter of the best answer.

FRANKIE	Oh, I can't understand it! The way it all just suddenly happened.
BERENICE	Happened? Happened?
FRANKIE	The whole thing. They are so beautiful.
BERENICE	(*After a pause*) I believe the sun done fried your brains.
JOHN HENRY	(*Whispering*) Me too.
BERENICE	You jealous. Go and behold yourself in the mirror. I can see from the color of your eyes. (*Frankie goes to the mirror and stares. She draws up her left shoulder, shakes her head, and turns away.*)
FRANKIE	(*With feeling*) Oh! They were the two prettiest people I ever saw. I just can't understand how it happened.

Transitional Note: Later that day Frankie makes up her mind to do something.

FRANKIE	(*Dreamily*) After the wedding I'm going with them to Winter Hill. I'm going off with them after the wedding.
JOHN HENRY	You serious?
FRANKIE	Shush, just now I realized something. The trouble with me is that for a long time I have been just an "I" person. All other people can say "we." When Berenice says "we" she means her lodge and church and colored people. Soldiers can say "we" and mean the army. All people belong to a "we" except me.
JOHN HENRY	What are we going to do?
FRANKIE	Not to belong to a "we" makes you too lonesome. Until this afternoon

	I didn't have a "we," but now after seeing Janice and Jarvis I suddenly realize something.
JOHN HENRY	What?
FRANKIE	I know that the bride and my brother are the "we" of me. So I'm going with them, and joining with the wedding.

Transitional Note: Frankie eagerly looks forward to the wedding. She buys a fancy dress and tells the whole town about her plans. In Act III, Janice and Jarvis get married. Afterward the couple comes to say good-bye.

JANICE	Darling, when we are settled we want you to come for a nice visit with us. But we don't yet have any place to live. (*She goes to Frankie and caresses her head. Frankie jerks.*) Won't you tell us good-bye now?
FRANKIE	(*With passion*) We! When you say we, you only mean you and Jarvis. And I am not included. (*She buries her head in her arms again and sobs.*)
	. . .
JOHN HENRY	They put Frankie out of the wedding. They hauled her out of the wedding car.
BERENICE	Don't tease your cousin, John Henry.
FRANKIE	It was a frame-up all around.
BERENICE	Well, don't bother no more about it. It's over now. Now cheer up.
FRANKIE	I wish the whole world would die.
BERENICE	School will begin now in only three more weeks and you'll find another bosom friend like Evelyn Owen you're so wild about.

1 Which of these is an <u>opinion</u> about Frankie?

A She is older than John Henry.

B She is jealous of Janice and Jarvis.

C She is disturbed by the news of the wedding.

D She plans to go away with the wedding couple.

2 "I believe the sun done fried your brains" is the author's way of saying that Frankie was

F acting strangely

G sunburned

H lonesome

J suffering

3 What did Frankie do just after the wedding?

A She gave the wedding couple a small gift.

B She got into the wedding couple's car and had to be removed.

C She tried to prevent the wedding couple from going away.

D She cried because her fancy dress looked ridiculous on her.

4 Frankie's comments about not belonging to a "we" show that she feels

F lonely

G superior

H angry

J pessimistic

5 In the scenes here, the author's purpose is probably to encourage the reader to

A see Frankie as silly

B feel empathy for Frankie

C feel admiration for Frankie

D see Frankie as a very unusual adolescent

6 Which of these is most likely to happen before the end of the play?

F Frankie will stop confiding in Berenice.

G Frankie will go live with Janice and Jarvis.

H Frankie will find another "we" to belong to.

J Frankie will go back to playing with John Henry.

7 Frankie's emotional state in the third excerpt could be described as

A happy

B nervous

C resigned

D miserable

8 Which conclusion can you draw about the play from these excerpts?

F It is about love.

G It is about growing up.

H It is about helping other people.

J It is about discovering your talents.

Check your answers on pages 66–67.

Practice 6 Usage

For numbers 1 through 8, read the passage and look at the numbered, underlined portions. Circle the answer that is written correctly for each underlined portion.

(1) Ida B. Wells, teacher, editor, and journalist, <u>were</u> a fearless and tireless crusader for equality and justice for African Americans. Born just before emancipation, she was the

(2) eldest of eight children. Nothing scared <u>she</u>. After her parents

(3) <u>die</u>, she reared her siblings, attended college, and became a

(4) <u>good</u> teacher than most.

As a newspaper editor and an orator, Wells crusaded against

(5) lynching, which had <u>increased alarming</u> during and after Reconstruction. She went on to help establish the NAACP, the nation's oldest civil rights organization. Wells continued to

(6) struggle for <u>she</u> people's rights until she died in 1931. African Americans, and

(7) indeed all Americans, <u>is</u> in debt to her for her ceaseless fight against injustice.

(8) People <u>will admire</u> Ida B. Wells forever.

1
A is
B was
C were being
D Correct as it is

2
F me   H hers
G her   J Correct as it is

3
A died
B dies
C are dying
D Correct as it is

4
F better
G gooder
H more good
J Correct as it is

5
A increased more alarmingly
B increased more alarming
C increased alarmingly
D Correct as it is

6
F he   H her
G his   J Correct as it is

7
A are
B were being
C has been
D Correct as it is

8
F admire
G admired
H are admiring
J Correct as it is

For numbers 9 through 11, circle the word or phrase that best completes the sentence.

9 Many authors _____ about Ida B. Wells over the years.

A write

B will write

C written

D have written

10 Wells _____ when she started an African American newspaper.

F teaches

G was teaching

H will be teaching

J has been teaching

11 Of all the issues on Wells' agenda, civil rights was fought for _____.

A extensivist

B extensively

C more extensively

D most extensively

For numbers 12 through 16, circle the sentence that is written correctly.

12 F Would you borrow me your book on Ida B. Wells?

G Do not lend my book on Ida B. Wells from me.

H May I borrow your book on Ida B. Wells?

J Sit the book on Ida B. Wells on the chair.

13 A There was never no one braver than she.

B Wells hadn't missed not a day of school.

C She wasn't scarcely never frightened.

D No one could scare Ida B. Wells.

14 F Wells is the most heroic woman I can imagine.

G Wells is the more heroic woman I can imagine.

H Wells is the most hero woman I can imagine.

J Wells is the heroicest woman I can imagine.

15 A Has there ever been a more remarkable person?

B Has there ever been a most remarkable person?

C Has there ever been a remarking person?

D Has there ever been a remarked person?

16 F A friend of mine read a biography of Wells because their teacher asked her to.

G Some people said he did not know why our housing project has her name.

H Two students chose Ida B. Wells when he wrote reports about a hero.

J I like to read about Wells because she is an interesting woman.

Check your answers on page 67.

Practice 7 | Sentence Formation

For numbers 1 through 3, read the underlined sentences. Then choose the sentence that best combines those sentences into one.

1 Everyone loves to shop at Greenacres Mall.
Greenacres Mall was remodeled five years ago.

   A Remodeled five years ago, everyone loves to shop at Greenacres Mall.
   B Greenacres Mall was remodeled five years ago, so everyone loves to shop there.
   C Everyone loves to shop at Greenacres Mall, which was remodeled five years ago.
   D Everyone loves to shop at Greenacres Mall because it was remodeled five years ago.

2 Her elder sister excels at mathematics and the hard sciences.
Hannah had no choice but to concentrate on literature, art, and music.

   F Her elder sister excels at mathematics and the hard sciences, Hannah had no choice but to concentrate on literature, art, and music.
   G Her elder sister excels at mathematics and the hard sciences, and Hannah had no choice but to concentrate on literature, art, and music.
   H Her elder sister excels at mathematics and the hard sciences, so Hannah had no choice but to concentrate on literature, art, and music.
   J Her elder sister excels at mathematics and the hard sciences, for Hannah had no choice but to concentrate on literature, art, and music.

3 Daniel wrote in his journal every day for many years.
Daniel wrote fluently in his journal.

   A Fluent Daniel wrote in his journal every day for many years.
   B Daniel wrote in his journal every day fluently for many years.
   C Daniel wrote fluently in his journal every day for many years.
   D Fluently, Daniel wrote in his journal every day for many years.

For numbers 4 through 6, read the paragraph and look at the numbered, underlined portions. Circle the answer that is written correctly for each underlined portion.

Since mortgage rates have decreased dramatically in recent months,
(4) everyone who has a mortgage should rush out and hurry to refinance, right?
(5) Wrong—or not necessarily right, There are several factors to consider. If your current mortgage rate is a percentage point or less higher than current rates, it may not be worth the cost of the refinancing fees. There are also income tax implications. Keep in mind that you will pay less interest with a lower mortgage rate, so your mortgage deduction will decrease. To figure out whether refinancing is the correct decision for you, search online for a mortgage
(6) calculator or having a consultation with a loan officer or an accountant.

4
F   rush and hurry out to refinance
G   rush and hurry to refinance
H   rush out to refinance
J   Correct as it is

5
A   right. There
B   right There
C   right there
D   Correct as it is

6
F   consult
G   going to consult
H   having a consult
J   Correct as it is

For numbers 7 through 12, circle the sentence that is written correctly.

7
A   A chest full of tools just bought Ricardo.
B   Ricardo just bought a chest full of tools.
C   People have lots of tools who like to use them.
D   Ricardo who was unpacking tools quickly called to us.

8
F   Amber often works long hours at her computer programming job frequently.
G   She is usually most often at her desk until 6:00 or 7:00.
H   Carey enjoys e-mailing her friends every day.
J   Carey is a hard worker who works really hard.

9
A   Taking too many breaks and talking on the phone too often.
B   Although she worked hard and arrived on time every day.
C   The fastest typist and the most pleasant person.
D   Cheri, our newest hire, is our best worker.

10
F   On most weekends we arise late, reading the paper, and eat pancakes.
G   Turn left at Main, go through two lights, and look for my house.
H   I like to shop, cook, and even washing and drying the dishes.
J   Begging, pleading, and pretend to cry won't work with me.

11
A   Wondering if their luggage would arrive safely, they left for the airport.
B   Pam brought presents for her neighbors that were expensive.
C   Before packing for the trip, the clothes were wrinkle free.
D   They packed the clothes with tissue paper between them.

12
F   Watch out for the ice, the roads are slippery today.
G   Though the weather is warmer, I suggest you wear a hat.
H   I've noticed how late it stays light in the afternoon, spring is coming!
J   I suppose Tomas will go sledding that's what he usually does after school.

Check your answers on pages 67–68.

Practice 8 Paragraph Development

For numbers 1 through 3, read the paragraph. Then choose the sentence that best fills the blank in the paragraph.

1 _____. Consider the temperament of the breed and the individual dog. Some dogs are too high strung to live with young children. Other dogs are just fine with family, but unfriendly to outsiders. Still others like people but may not interact well with other dogs. Another issue is physical characteristics. Dogs may drool, shed, and knock things over with their tails. Some require constant grooming; others need massive amounts of exercise. Yes, the dog search is challenging, but the rewards can be great!

A   Taking care of a dog requires plenty of work.

B   There are hundreds of different breeds of dogs.

C   Finding the perfect dog for your family can be a challenge.

D   A dog show is a good place to examine all the different dog breeds.

2 The Mexican artist Frida Kahlo was a unique human being and artist whose life and work left a lasting legacy. Most of her small jewel-like paintings were self-portraits. _____. Kahlo's stormy marriage to the renowned muralist Diego Rivera, her radical politics, and her bond with the Mexican people also informed her art—and her life. Born just after the Mexican Revolution, she died in 1954, just days after appearing at a protest rally.

F   Kahlo was just 47 when she died.

G   Kahlo divorced and remarried Diego.

H   Kahlo and Rivera spent time together in the U. S., where Rivera painted murals.

J   Many related to a horrible bus accident she had suffered and to her miscarriages.

3 Tying education funding to state lotteries is a big mistake. Do we really want the state to endorse gambling and the host of illegal activities that accompany it? What do our children gather about the value of education if education is funded in such a way? And, above all, the fluctuating funds available from the lottery make planning for education spending difficult at best. _____.

A   Surely, our children deserve better.

B   For instance, our children deserve better.

C   Likewise, our children deserve better.

D   Unfortunately, our children deserve better.

For numbers 4 and 5, read the paragraph. Then circle the sentence that does not belong in the paragraph.

4 1. To cook perfect pasta, fill a heavy pot with plenty of water. 2. Then add salt and bring the water to a full boil. 3. Some people like red sauce best, but others prefer clam sauce. 4. Put in the pasta, stir so it doesn't stick together, and cook until it is al dente—which means a bit chewy.

F   Sentence 1

G   Sentence 2

H   Sentence 3

J   Sentence 4

5 1. It's not hard to give a great party if you invite old friends and mix in some new people. 2. Have plenty of good food, but don't spend all your time in the kitchen. 3. Alan and Gretchen give the best parties of anyone I know! 4. Finally, stay relaxed, and make sure everyone is comfortable together.

A   Sentence 1

B   Sentence 2

C   Sentence 3

D   Sentence 4

For numbers 6 and 7, circle the answer that best develops the topic sentence.

6 There are good reasons that Chicago became the birthplace of the skyscraper.

F   Chicago has dozens of famous high-rise buildings.

G   In the late 1800s, Chicago was a bustling commercial city.

H   After the Chicago fire of 1871, the entire city was rebuilt.

J   Today, though, Chicago has lost its reputation for architectural innovation.

7 Star athletes deserve every dollar of the millions they earn.

A   They are coddled and shielded from the real world.

B   Some star athletes use performance-enhancing drugs.

C   They make even more millions for club owners, leagues, and cities.

D   Every professional athlete deserves the salary that he or she receives.

Check your answers on page 68.

For numbers 1 through 5, read the passage and look at the numbered, underlined portions. Circle the answer that is written correctly for each underlined portion.

(1) More than a century later, the words of designer <u>John a. Roebling's</u> still describe

(2) the Brooklyn Bridge best. He said it was the greatest bridge in existence. This <u>grand Suspension bridge</u> was the world's first to be suspended from steel cables and was

(3) 50% longer than any previous suspension bridge. Read about the <u>Brooklyn Bridge</u>

(4) in <u>*Great Bridge: The Epic Story of the Building of the Brooklyn Bridge*</u> by

(5) <u>David mcCullough.</u>

1 A John A. Roebling
   B John A. roebling
   C john a. Roebling
   D Correct as it is

2 F Grand Suspension Bridge
   G Grand suspension bridge
   H grand suspension bridge
   J Correct as it is

3 A brooklyn Bridge
   B Brooklyn bridge
   C brooklyn bridge
   D Correct as it is

4 F *great bridge: The Epic Story of the Building of the Brooklyn Bridge*
   G *Great Bridge: The Epic Story of the Building of the Brooklyn bridge*
   H *Great Bridge: The Epic Story Of The Building of the Brooklyn Bridge*
   J Correct as it is

5 A david mccullough
   B david McCullough
   C David McCullough
   D Correct as it is

For numbers 6 through 13, circle the sentence that is written correctly <u>and</u> shows the correct capitalization. Be sure the sentence you choose is complete.

6
F The madonna concert is at Van Andel auditorium.

G Grandmother's favorite movie is *Gone with the Wind*.

H Would you like to be a Physical Therapist or a Paramedic?

J Ana remembers each of her teachers' names from ms. Tang to mr. Verdon.

7
A The least visited National Park is Isle Royale National Park.

B Isle Royale National Park is an island in Lake Superior.

C kayla and Keegan camped there last Summer.

D You can take the ferry *royal crown* there.

8
F People say Dr. Ruiz is so gentle that they don't mind visiting the dentist.

G He has *people* magazine to read and posters on the ceiling above the dental chair.

H I was still nervous as I waited in the waiting room to see dr. Ruiz.

J He is the newest and youngest dentist in the greater fruitport area.

9
A The new Middle School in Treetorn finally opened this year.

B The school will be open all year, even during the Summer.

C Classes like "Intro to Lifesaving" will be held in summer.

D I think J. p. Morgan will teach that class.

10
F Have you been to Scoops, the new ice cream store?

G Wally White and his Family manage it.

H Wally makes Dozens of great flavors.

J You can order Waffle Cones, too.

11
A Tryouts for this year's school play, *our Town*, are next Tuesday.

B The triplets Billy, bobby, and Brian will surely try out.

C The play might have to be held downtown at the Uptown theater.

D The auditorium at W.E.B. Du Bois High School is being remodeled.

12
F Gary had always wanted to be a Veterinarian.

G He was accepted to Michigan State's program.

H The vet program at Michigan state is really tough.

J But all the Smiths know how to work hard, so gary will do fine.

13
A The job of College Professor doesn't get the respect it deserves.

B Have you read *the Fountainhead* by Ayn Rand?

C Don't forget to turn left on Greene boulevard.

D Next summer, let's visit the Grand Canyon.

Check your answers on pages 68–69.

For numbers 1 and 2, circle the answer that shows which punctuation mark, if any, is needed in the sentence.

1 The only books DeWan reads are mysteries mysteries, and more mysteries.

A ?   B ,   C .   D None

2 Did she say, "Please pass the bread"?

F ,   G .   H ;   J None

For number 3, circle the sentence that is complete and written correctly and shows the proper capitalization and punctuation.

3
A Adele Smythe was a most generous donor; her son carries on that tradition.
B Tanya likes the red, tea-length gown: Sara prefers the slinky black dress.
C Grommet always fetches slippers, and fetches everything else, too.
D If Martha calls before 8:00 she's sure to find David at home.

For numbers 4 through 8, read the paragraph and look at the numbered, underlined portions. Circle the answer that is written correctly for each underlined portion.

(4) Naturally a successful garage sale requires the proper
(5) preparation. Before you have a garage sale, it goes without saying you need to know what prices are like in your area. Check
(6) some garage sales around town; How are the items displayed?
(7) What categories of merchandise move most quickly? And finally, as I mentioned, what are prices for items similar to what you
(8) plan to sell? Once you've done your homework; advertised, and displayed the merchandise attractively, you're ready for business!

Garage Sale
Sat. & Sun.
8am – 5pm
furniture, antiques

4 F Naturally, a
G Naturally; a
H Naturally, A
J Correct as it is

6 F town: how
G town, how
H town. How
J Correct as it is

5 A sale it goes without saying
B sale it goes without saying,
C sale, it goes without saying,
D Correct as it is

7 A finally as I mentioned,
B finally, as I mentioned
C finally; as I mentioned;
D Correct as it is

8 F homework; advertised, and displayed the merchandise attractively

    G homework; advertised, and displayed the merchandise attractively

    H homework, advertised, and displayed the merchandise attractively,

    J Correct as it is

For numbers 9 through 13, read the paragraph and look at the numbered, underlined portions. Circle the answer that is written correctly for each underlined portion.

(9)   Jan works as an <u>aid, also called a tester,</u> for the Fair Housing Commission.

(10) She and a partner try to rent <u>apartments apply for mortgages and so on.</u>

(11) <u>As you know Jan</u> is Caucasian, and her testing partner

(12) is either <u>Caucasian, Hispanic, or African</u> American.

(13) <u>Surprisingly she</u> hasn't found discrimination in some of the

       places she expected to.

9 A aid also called a tester

    B aid, also called a tester

    C aid also called a tester,

    D Correct as it is

10 F apartments, apply for mortgages and so on.

    G apartments: apply for mortgages, and so on.

    H apartments, apply for mortgages, and so on.

    J Correct as it is

11 A As you know Jan,

    B As you know, Jan

    C As you know, Jan,

    D Correct as it is

12 F Caucasian; Hispanic, or African

    G Caucasian, Hispanic or African

    H Caucasian Hispanic, or African

    J Correct as it is

13 A Surprisingly: she

    B Surprisingly; she

    C Surprisingly, she

    D Correct as it is

Check your answers on page 69.

For numbers 1 through 5, read the letter and look at the numbered, underlined portions. Circle the answer that is written correctly for each underlined portion.

(1)   August 20 2004

Rice Bix Company
(2)   320; Cereal Boulevard
(3)   Battle Creek, MI 49417

(4)   Dear Sir or Madam

In these busy days, we rarely stop to give a compliment. Well, I would like to stop to give your company a compliment. Rice Bix is a really delicious cereal. My family, including the dog, loves your product. We also appreciate the reasonable price. Thanks!

(5)   Sincerely yours

                                             Flora Simonian
                                             Flora Simonian

1   A   August, 20 2004
    B   August 20, 2004
    C   August 20; 2004
    D   Correct as it is

2   F   320 Cereal Boulevard
    G   320, Cereal Boulevard
    H   320 Cereal, Boulevard
    J   Correct as it is

3   A   Battle Creek MI 49417
    B   Battle Creek MI, 49417
    C   Battle Creek, MI, 49417
    D   Correct as it is

4   F   Dear Sir or Madam:
    G   Dear Sir or Madam.
    H   Dear Sir, or Madam,
    J   Correct as it is

5   A   Sincerely, yours
    B   Sincerely yours,
    C   Sincerely yours;
    D   Correct as it is

For numbers 6 through 8, read the passage and look at the numbered, underlined portions. Circle the answer that is written correctly for each underlined portion.

(6)   We didn't have much money when I grew up in <u>Squamish, Ohio,</u> so I really

(7) admired my <u>sisters'</u> skill with a sewing machine. She would look at a picture

(8) in a magazine and <u>say "I</u> can copy that." And she would. Guess who grew up to

    be a fashion designer?

6 F Squamish Ohio,

    G Squamish, Ohio

    H Squamish, Ohio;

    J Correct as it is

8 F say. "I

    G say; "I

    H say, "I

    J Correct as it is

7 A sisters   C sisterses'

    B sister's   D Correct as it is

For numbers 9 and 10, circle the sentence that is complete and written correctly and shows the proper capitalization and punctuation.

9 A "What will we get for Sean's birthday"? asked Zooey.

    B "Well," I paused a moment, "There's always a gift certificate."

    C "Oh, come on! Surely, we can do better than that, Zooey replied."

    D "Maybe we can get some ideas from this catalogue, I" sighed thoughtfully.

10 F "We could go to Woodland Mall" Zooey remarked.

    G "I hate shopping!" I said to Zooey.

    H "Don't have a fit." she replied.

    J Get out the catalogue," I said.

For numbers 11 through 14, decide which punctuation mark, if any, is needed in the sentence.

11 "Who's your favorite author? Marta asked Hayley.

    A ?   B ,   C "   D None

12 "That depends on my mood," Hayley replied.

    F ?   G ,   H "   J None

13 "When I'm feeling gloomy," she added, "I love fantasy"

    A ?   B .   C "   D None

14 "And when I'm cheerful, I love to read fiction," she said, laughing.

    F ?   G ,   H "   J None

Check your answers on pages 69–70.

Practice 12 Vowel

For numbers 1 through 8, circle the word that is spelled correctly.

1 _____ show that women live longer than men.

A Stitistics

B Statistics

C Stutistics

D Stetistics

2 The employer made _____ inquiries about his behavior at work.

F discret

G discreit

H discreet

J discreat

3 Marta has never had any political _____.

A asperations

B asparations

C aspirations

D aspurations

4 I had to _____ in the argument between Jack and John.

F intervene

G intervine

H interveine

J interveene

5 He has a _____ point.

A valud

B vallud

C valid

D vallid

6 I have made many _____ contributions this year.

F charitable

G charitibel

H charitabel

J chariteble

7 We need to devise a _____ way of organizing our files.

A sistematic

B sistamatic

C systematic

D systamatic

8 The letter was written with _____.

F brevety

G brevity

H brevitey

J brevetey

Check your answers on page 70.

Practice 13 Consonant

For numbers 1 through 8, circle the word that is spelled correctly.

1 Did you _____ which flavor you want?

A   spesify

B   specify

C   spessify

D   spescify

2 It is important to be _____.

F   imparcial

G   imparsial

H   impartial

J   imparshal

3 Joshua is a _____ skier.

A   novise

B   novice

C   novisce

D   noviss

4 Tom Stoppard is an accomplished _____.

F   playwrite

G   playrite

H   playright

J   playwright

5 He gained _____ to the building.

A   acess

B   acses

C   access

D   acces

6 The _____ department can handle your vacation request.

F   personel

G   personell

H   personnel

J   presonnell

7 I am very _____ to catching colds.

A   susseptable

B   suseptible

C   suseptable

D   susceptible

8 Most of the _____ papers in *Cell Biology* are well researched and well written.

F   siantific

G   syantific

H   scientific

J   sientific

Check your answers on page 70.

For numbers 1 through 8, circle the word that is spelled correctly and best completes the sentence.

1 Bob went to the _____ store to buy a birthday card for his wife.

A stationary

B stashunary

C stationery

D stationerry

2 There is no _____ for a decision like this.

F precedent

G presedent

H precedant

J presedant

3 Management has taken _____ measures to improve the situation.

A expedent

B expediant

C expedient

D expedeint

4 I've never been afraid of thunder and _____.

F lietening

G litening

H lightning

J lightening

5 Your great idea has rapidly gained _____.

A acceptanse

B acceptense

C acceptance

D acceptence

6 Public _____ about the disease is a cause for concern.

F ignorance

G ignorence

H ignoreance

J ignoreanse

7 The _____ had dinner with the Secretary of State.

A ambasadar

B ambassader

C ambasader

D ambassador

8 She wasn't very _____ about sharing information.

F scrupulous

G scrupulus

H scrupeulus

J scrupuelous

Check your answers on pages 70–71.

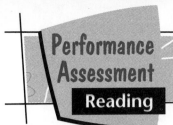
The Reading Performance Assessment is identical to the real TABE in format and in length. It will give you an idea of what the real test is like. Allow yourself 50 minutes to complete this assessment. Check your answers on pages 71–74.

Sample A

The house was dark, so Levi turned on the _____.

A   oven

B   radio

C   lights

D   computer

Sample B

Marla left the party suddenly. Her brother had just phoned. His car had broken down at a rest stop. She wanted to help him.

Why did Marla leave the party?

F   Her car had broken down.

G   Her phone wasn't working.

H   She wasn't having a good time.

J   She wanted to help her brother.

This passage is adapted from "The Gift of the Magi," a story by O. Henry. The story takes place over a hundred years ago. Read the passage. Then answer questions 1 through 6 by circling the letter of the best answer.

Della counted the small pile of coins on the table one more time. They totaled one dollar and eighty-seven cents. Tomorrow was Christmas, and it was all she had to buy a present for her husband Jim, after scrimping and saving for months. She looked around the familiar, shabby apartment and began to cry.

Della had hoped to buy something fine and well made for Jim, something worthy of his character. It should be made of silver, she thought. Suddenly she had an idea. She pulled the comb out of her long beautiful brown hair and let it fall. It was her prized possession, and Jim loved it. The only thing that the couple treasured as much was the gold watch that had belonged to Jim's father and grandfather. With a tear in her eye, Della headed for a little shop nearby, Madame Sofronie's Hair Goods of All Kinds.

"Twenty dollars," Madame Sofronie said. Della nodded.

Two hours later, Della was delighted to find the perfect gift for Jim—a simple, finely crafted silver chain for his cherished watch. It cost her twenty-one dollars.

That night, Della waited excitedly for Jim to come home from work. She had done her best to make her short hair look pretty. As Jim stepped into the house, he looked thin and very serious. He was only twenty-two and already burdened with a family. He had no gloves and desperately needed a new overcoat.

Jim fixed his gaze on Della, but she couldn't make out what he was thinking. She began to explain. "I just couldn't go through Christmas without giving you something nice." He was too good-natured and in love with her to be angry.

Jim embraced Della warmly. Then he pulled out a small package from his overcoat. "Don't worry, Dell. But if you unwrap this, you'll see why I was a little stunned." Della tore off the wrapping and let out a squeal of joy. Then she began to sob. She held in her hands the pure tortoise-shell combs with jeweled rims she had long admired in a Broadway window.

Jim comforted her. At last she looked up and smiled. "My hair grows so fast, Jim," she said. Then she thought of her present for him. She held out the handsome watch chain in her palm. "Try it," she said eagerly.

Jim sank back onto the couch and smiled. "I sold my watch to get money to buy your combs." Then he suggested that they put their nice presents away for a while and sit down to enjoy their Christmas supper.

1 The first paragraph of the passage contains the phrase "after *scrimping* and saving for months." What does the word *scrimping* mean?

A studying hard

B spending little

C standing firmly

D searching thoroughly

2 Which of these does not support the idea that Della and Jim are poor?

F Jim and Della's apartment was shabby.

G Della wanted to buy Jim something fine.

H Della had been able to save only $1.87 for a present.

J Jim had no gloves to wear in winter and only a worn-out overcoat.

3 In the third paragraph of the passage, "Della nodded" is the author's way of saying that Della

A had found just the right gift for Jim

B went through with her plan to sell her hair

C knew that Jim was not angry about her hair

D wanted a higher price from Madame Sofronie for her hair

4 Jim's gift showed that he was

F not willing to spend a lot of money

G determined to get Della an impractical gift

H willing to make a sacrifice

J determined to purchase a gift as fine as the gift Della purchased for him

5 Which of these best summarizes the passage?

A People in love often act foolishly.

B Generosity and love are the best gifts.

C Poor people can find a way to buy presents.

D Beautiful gifts are the most likely to please.

6 Which of these is most likely to happen next in the story?

F Jim and Della will get a divorce.

G Jim and Della will have three children.

H Jim and Della will keep and eventually use their gifts.

J Jim and Della will return the gifts to get their money back.

The numbers on this map show two police precincts in the same community. Each precinct has a separate police station to serve the area. Study the map and read the information about the map. Then answer questions 7 through 11 by circling the letter of the best answer.

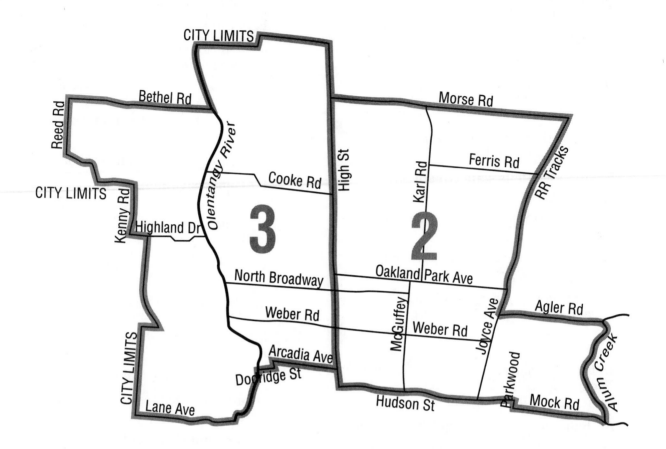

How to Find the Police Precinct in Which You Live

1. Each precinct has a number.

2. Read the map to find your street.

3. On the street, find the approximate location of where you live.

4. A bold line shows the boundaries of the precinct.

5. Find the bold lines around the spot where you live.

6. Look for the bold number in the center of that precinct.

7 This precinct map is useful for

    A finding out where to shop

    B finding out where to vote

    C contacting the right police station

    D locating the right elementary school

8 Marlene knows she lives on Weber Road, but she can't remember what precinct she lives in. What else does she need to know from the map to find out what her precinct is?

    F which side of High Street she lives on

    G which side of Alum Creek she lives on

    H which side of Morse Road she lives on

    J whether she lives within the city limits

9 According to the map, one boundary of precinct 3 is

    A Ferris Road

    B Cooke Road

    C Bethel Road

    D North Broadway

10 If Lorenzo moves from Highland Drive to the corner of Oakland Park Avenue and McGuffy, what precinct will he live in?

    F precinct 1

    G precinct 2

    H precinct 3

    J precinct 4

11 According to the map, which road lies partly in precinct 2 and partly in precinct 3?

    A Reed Road

    B Joyce Avenue

    C Highland Drive

    D North Broadway

Performance Assessment: Reading

This passage is about "affirmative action." Read the passage and the letter to the editor. Then answer questions 12 through 19 by circling the letter of the best answer.

The Civil Rights Act of 1964 outlawed discrimination in the workplace based on race. In response to this law, the federal government began a policy of affirmative action. The aim of this policy was to correct the effects of past discrimination by creating more job opportunities for African Americans. Later, affirmative action was extended to other minorities and women.

Affirmative action can take many forms. One example is a company program that favors the hiring of minority applicants. Another example is a state government that requires setting aside a certain number of road construction projects for minority-owned businesses.

In the 1970s, many colleges and universities adopted affirmative action policies. For example, the University of California decided to reserve 16 out of 100 places for minority students when admitting new students. In 1978, Allan Bakke challenged the University of California's policy. Bakke was denied admission to the medical school. He sued the university after discovering that an African-American applicant with lower test scores had been accepted.

In the landmark Bakke case, the Supreme Court ruled that numerical quotas, or set-asides, were illegal because they did not treat all citizens equally. At the same time, the Court stated that race could be a "plus factor" in making admissions or hiring decisions in public institutions. In support of this position, the court stated that creating a diverse campus was a "compelling" benefit to society. Recent decades have seen additional challenges to affirmative action programs, especially those based on race.

To the editor:

Affirmative-action programs in college admissions have sparked an emotional debate. Some opponents say that schools should never give preference to minorities based on race. They argue that preferential treatment results in "reverse discrimination" if qualified applicants are bypassed in favor of less qualified applicants. Others stress that the African-American middle class has expanded in the past 20 years. Affirmative-action programs, therefore, should focus on low-income students of any race.

Supporters say that efforts to achieve a diverse student body have not led to the admission of unqualified students. They point out that most admissions policies give many more points to academic factors, such as test scores and grades, than to race. Supporters also argue that affirmative-action programs have worked. They have opened doors for many disadvantaged members of society.

Both sides make important points. Affirmative action has been successful, but discrimination still exists in our society. Therefore, creating a racially mixed environment on campuses is still a worthy goal. If race still matters, though, it matters more for some students than others. A program based on need is the fairest. Affirmative-action programs must consider both merit and economic need and treat each student individually.

Sincerely,

Cesar Sullivan

---

12 In the fourth paragraph of the passage, the word *compelling* in the phrase "*compelling* benefit to society" means

F slight   **H** important

G limiting   **J** contradictory

13 Which piece of evidence from the passage shows that colleges in the past used quotas in making admissions decisions?

A The Supreme Court said that race could be a "plus factor" in college admissions.

B The government awarded a certain number of construction projects to minority businesses.

C The Civil Rights Law of 1964 made racial discrimination in the workplace illegal.

D The University of California set aside 16 out of 100 admissions places for minorities.

14 Which of these statements from the letter to the editor does not express an opinion?

F A needs-based program is the fairest.

G The African-American middle class has expanded in the past 20 years.

H Creating a racially mixed environment on campuses is still a worthy goal.

J Affirmative action programs should focus on low-income students of any race.

15 According to some who are against affirmative action programs, "reverse discrimination" refers to the unfair treatment of

A qualified applicants

B blacks

C women

D Hispanics

16 According to the passage, the Supreme Court compared numerical quotas to

F reverse discrimination

G traditional discrimination

H equal opportunity

J unequal treatment

17 What evidence of unfair treatment did Allan Bakke cite in his lawsuit against the University of California?

A Only minority students were admitted in the year that he applied.

B The quota system at the university favored the acceptance of white students.

C He was not allowed to graduate because of his lawsuit against the university.

D An African-American applicant with lower test scores had been accepted, while he was rejected.

18 Which of these events happened first?

F Allan Bakke sued the University of California.

G The Supreme Court declared that racial quotas were illegal.

H The Civil Rights Act outlawed discrimination in the workplace.

J Allan Bakke applied to the medical school at the University of California.

19 In paragraph 2 of the letter to the editor, the word *body* in the phrase "student *body*" refers to

A a group of persons

B the firmness of something

C the main part of a written work

D the physical substance of a human being

Read this passage about an organization called Habitat for Humanity. Then answer questions 20 through 25 by circling the letter of the best answer.

In Hawaii, a family with six children lives in nothing but a tent on the beach for years. In California, a family living in a dilapidated public housing project witnesses violent gang activity on an almost daily basis. In Philadelphia, a mother and daughter rent an apartment where the walls and ceilings are crumbling from water leaks and only one bedroom is fit to sleep in.

These are just three examples of the 2.6 million American families who do not have adequate housing. In addition to these are some 8 million families who can only pay for their housing by going without food, clothing, and other basic needs. These families spend at least half of their income just on shelter.

Creating decent shelter for people like these is the goal of Habitat for Humanity International (HFHI). HFHI, a nonprofit organization, seeks to eliminate poverty housing and homelessness around the world.

Why does a housing problem exist? The main reason is the gap between wages and the cost of heating, lighting, and maintaining an apartment or house. In many families, wage earners do not have the skills or education to find a good-paying job. Severe illness and unemployment can compound the problem, leaving people homeless or with no choice but to move to rundown or unsafe housing. While low incomes are one side of the problem, the diminishing supply of well-maintained, affordable housing is another part of the problem.

Using volunteer workers and donations of money and building supplies, HFHI builds and upgrades simple, decent houses with the help of the homeowner families. The houses are sold to the families at no profit and financed with no-interest loans. A key feature of the program is that homeowners must invest many hours of their own labor. They are required to take part in building their Habitat house as well as the houses of others.

A typical Habitat house is modest in size. It is big enough for the family's needs and but small enough to keep building and maintenance costs low. Locally available building materials are used. Houses generally have a wood frame, Gypsum-board interior walls, vinyl siding, and asphalt shingle roofs. Experienced staff supervise the construction and train volunteers and partner families to help with the construction.

People who apply for a Habitat house are seeking a better life for their families. Habitat partners gain self-esteem and comfort in knowing they will always have a roof over their heads. As one Habitat partner said, "I don't have to be ashamed of where I live. I'm going to live the rest of my life in a wonderful home. From this point on, it's all up to me."

20 Someone who volunteers for Habitat for Humanity probably has a desire to

   F clean up pollution in the environment

   G assist others in obtaining decent housing

   H educate others so they can get better jobs

   J improve the appearance of their neighborhood

21 The portrayal of an apartment "where the walls and ceilings are crumbling from water leaks" is the author's way of describing

   A the conditions in which the homeless live

   B the poor housing situation one family faced

   C a typical Habitat for Humanity project

   D well-maintained, affordable housing

22 According to the passage, what is most likely true about people who apply for a Habitat house?

   F They want decent and affordable housing.

   G They are unemployed.

   H They are lazy.

   J They have a high standard of living.

23 Based on what you have learned in this passage, you can predict that

   A Habitat projects are supervised by trained staff

   B a wealthy person would not qualify to get a Habitat house

   C volunteers help to build habitat houses for those who need them

   D homeowners must do some of the work on the house themselves

24 The passage states that "the *diminishing* supply of well-maintained, affordable housing" is part of the problem. Which of these means the opposite of the word *diminishing,* as used in this phrase?

   F large

   G small

   H growing

   J decreasing

25 The author's main purpose in writing this passage is to

   A urge people to volunteer for Habitat projects

   B provide an introduction to Habitat for Humanity

   C criticize the activities of Habitat for Humanity

   D discuss the problem of homelessness in the United States

Study the form and read the paragraph. Then answer questions 26 through 30 by circling the letter of the best answer.

Margaret Koso, who is a 29-year-old secretary, will be out of the country on the day of the next general election for president, but she wants to vote. She can arrange to do this by filling out the application for an absentee voter's ballot below. This form allows her to submit her vote without going to the "polling place" or building where she normally votes.

APPLICATION FOR ABSENT VOTER'S BALLOT

Return to Greene County Board of Elections

(PLEASE TYPE OR PRINT)

SEND BALLOTS TO:
(if different from home address)

Applicant's Name————————————

Name————————————

Home Address————————————

Care of /P.O.Box————————————

City, Village, or Post Office————————————

Address————————————

County———— Zip Code————————

City———— State——— Zip Code————

I wish to vote in the following election: (check only one)

1. PRIMARY ELECTION: ___Democratic   ___Republican   ___Other Party (specify)————

2. ___ GENERAL ELECTION   3. ___SPECIAL ELECTION   ELECTION DATE————

I will be absent from my polling place for the following reason: (you must check one)

1.___ I am sixty-two years of age or older.
2.___ I will be out of the country on election day. (Applicants who will be outside of the United States must also check the appropriate box on the enclosed return envelope to indicate that they will be outside the country.)
3.___ Due to physical illness, disability, or infirmity.
      ___(I request the assistance of two election officials.)
4.___ Due to a hospital admission for medical or surgical treatment for me or a family member.
5.___ I am an election official or an employee of the Secretary of State.
6.___ I am a full-time fire fighter, peace officer, or emergency medical services provider.
7.___ Due to observance of my religious beliefs.
8.___ I am in active duty with the organized militia in the State of Ohio.
9.___ I am confined to a public or private institution within the county. Please have two board employees deliver my ballot.
10.___ Due to my confinement in jail or workhouse under sentence for a misdemeanor or waiting trial on a felony or misdemeanor.
11.___ I am a former resident entitled to vote for President and Vice President.

I am a qualified elector and request an absentee ballot for the above reason.

VOTER SIGNATURE ————————————— DATE————

NOTE: THIS APPLICATION MUST BE COMPLETELY FILLED OUT AND SIGNED TO BE PROCESSED !!

---

1. Use of this form is optional. Application must include name, voter residence address, reason for absence from polls, applicant's signature, election for which ballots are requested and if primary ballots, voters party affiliation.
2. An application by mail must be received by the Board of Elections by noon on the third day before the election. Applications by the voter in person may be received until the close of regular board hours the day before the election. Applications for persons who are hospitalized by a medical emergency will be accepted until 3:00 p.m. on election day.
3. Completed ballots must be delivered to the Board of Elections in person, by mail, or a near relative not later than the close of polls on election day. Exception: If the voter is outside of the United States on election day, the ballot envelope must be signed and postmarked prior to the close of the polls and received by the Board of Elections not later than 10 days after the election or 20 days after the presidential primary election.
4. If you request an absentee ballot, you will not be allowed to vote or turn in your ballot at the polling place on election day.
5. This document may be reproduced.

26 In the list under "I will be absent from my polling place for the following reason," Ms. Koso should check

    F line 1

    G line 2

    H line 7

    J line 8

27 All of the following are acceptable reasons for being absent from the polling place on election day <u>except</u>

    A a hospital admission

    B illness, disability, or infirmity

    C being sixty-two years old or older

    D confinement in jail due to conviction of a felony

28 Under "I wish to vote in the following election," Ms. Koso should check

    F other party

    G special election

    H general election

    J primary election

29 If Ms. Koso decides to mail in her application form to the Board of Elections, by when must it be received?

    A by 3:00 p.m. on election day

    B not later than ten days after the election

    C by noon on the third day before the election

    D by the close of the regular board hours on the day before the election

30 Ms. Koso most likely received this form from

    F a company supervisor

    G the post office

    H the Department of Motor Vehicles

    J the Board of Elections

Read this passage about Colin Powell. Then answer questions 31 through 37 by circling the letter of the best answer.

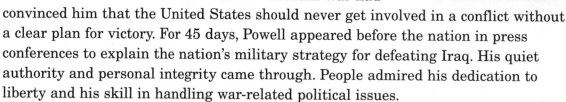

Colin Powell has demonstrated his leadership in a career that has spanned four decades and includes top positions in both the military and the White House. In 1989 President George H. W. Bush appointed him to the nation's highest military office, chairman of the Joint Chiefs of Staff. He was the youngest man and the first African American to hold this job. The chairman's role is to keep communication open between the military and the Administration and to supervise military spending. In times of war, the chairman draws up plans for military action.

Powell oversaw Operation Desert Storm. This was the U.S. military response in 1991 to Iraq's invasion of Kuwait, known as the Gulf War. Powell's service in the Vietnam War had convinced him that the United States should never get involved in a conflict without a clear plan for victory. For 45 days, Powell appeared before the nation in press conferences to explain the nation's military strategy for defeating Iraq. His quiet authority and personal integrity came through. People admired his dedication to liberty and his skill in handling war-related political issues.

Powell retired from the U.S. Army in 1993. Despite pressure to run for high office, Powell chose to stay out of the political arena. In 1997, he founded an organization called America's Promise. This group emphasizes the presence of caring parents, mentors, tutors, and coaches in helping young people develop.

Powell, the son of Jamaican immigrants, credits his own success to the strong support he received from his parents. He was raised in a working-class neighborhood in New York's South Bronx. In his family there was an expectation to do better. Among his cousins are a federal judge, a foreign ambassador, a psychologist, and a successful businessman. As chairman of America's Promise, Powell urges volunteers to challenge young people by having high expectations of them.

Powell settled on a military career at an early age. While attending the City College of New York, he joined the Reserve Officers' Training Corps (ROTC). In the 1960s, he served in South Vietnam and was awarded two Purple Hearts and other medals.

After returning home from Vietnam, Powell earned a master's degree in business administration in 1971. The next year he was awarded a White House fellowship in the Office of Management and Budget. This was the first of several political positions Powell took over the next 15 years as he advanced his military career. These jobs helped him sharpen his political skills and understand the Washington bureaucracy.

In 2001, Powell returned to politics as Secretary of State under President George W. Bush. He was the first African American ever to hold this position. As Secretary of State, the president's key advisor on foreign policy, Powell has remained committed to the principle of helping any country that wishes to become democratic.

31 Which event threw Colin Powell into the public spotlight?

   A his role in the Vietnam War

   B his appointment as a federal judge

   C the publication of his autobiography

   D his handling of Operation Desert Storm

32 This passage would most likely be found in a

   F book describing the Gulf War

   G training manual for Army officers

   H collection of profiles of famous African Americans

   J book describing the inside workings of the White House

33 Which of these conclusions about Powell can be drawn from the passage?

   A He has always wanted to inspire and train new soldiers.

   B He has always been concerned with the negative effects of racism.

   C He has a deep understanding of energy and budget issues.

   D He has high expectations of himself and of others.

34 Which of the following most likely led Colin Powell to found America's Promise?

   F his ROTC training

   G Operation Desert Storm

   H the example set by his parents

   J his White House fellowship

35 Which of these statements about Colin Powell is <u>not</u> supported by information in the passage?

   A He has little interest in politics.

   B He feels a sense of duty to his country.

   C He is committed to helping America's youth.

   D He served courageously in the Vietnam War.

36 Which of these best summarizes the passage?

   F A dedicated soldier rises to the rank of general.

   G A disadvantaged youth overcomes great obstacles.

   H An African American shows a lifelong commitment to young people.

   J An African American, with a military background, becomes a national leader.

37 Which of the following is a <u>fact</u> about Colin Powell?

   A He would make an excellent president.

   B He was the best military planner in the U.S. Army.

   C He is the most admired African American alive.

   D He decided on a military career while in college.

This passage is about a new kind of car. Read the passage. Then answer questions 38 through 44 by circling the letter of the best answer.

A new technology may revolutionize the way we drive in the twenty-first century. Automotive scientists have been working to develop a car powered by hydrogen rather than gasoline. The power plant in a hydrogen car is a fuel cell rather than an internal-combustion engine (ICE). The fuel cell converts hydrogen gas into electricity, which powers the car.

Petroleum-based fuel powers conventional engines. This fuel is burned up inside the car and the byproducts—including carbon dioxide, carbon monoxide, and nitrogen oxides—are emitted as exhaust. All of these substances cause pollution in the environment.

Cars powered by hydrogen fuel cells would be much more environmentally friendly. Hydrogen fuel cells generate power by splitting hydrogen atoms into parts called electrons and protons. The electrons drive the motor that powers the car. Only water and heat are emitted as byproducts. Hydrogen-powered cars are nearly twice as efficient as ICE cars. Furthermore, petroleum fuels come from oil supplies in the earth that are rapidly being used up. Hydrogen gas, in contrast, can be extracted from many energy sources, including natural gas, ethanol, and water.

Switching from gasoline- to hydrogen-powered vehicles, however, raises a chicken-and-egg problem. New kinds of power plants will be needed to generate hydrogen, as well as pipelines to distribute it. These will not be built, however, until there are large numbers of fuel-cell vehicles on the road. Developing the required infrastructure will require public education, support from local and national leaders, and funding for research and demonstration projects.

Hydrogen-powered cars look quite different from the cars we know. The steering, brakes, and throttle controls are all controlled electronically. Thus there is no bulky engine compartment, no awkward hump running down the middle of the car, and no steering wheel or pedals to control the gas and brakes. The fuel cells, along with the fuel tanks, heating system, and radiator, fit into a "skateboard" chassis. This flat chassis makes the cabin interior much roomier than in ICE vehicles and allows for the creation of unique body styles. In fact, car owners in the future might be able to "plug in" different tops on the same chassis, creating a family sedan or a luxury car as needed.

38 The passage states that hydrogen-powered cars have a "skateboard *chassis*." The word *chassis* refers to a vehicle's

F frame

G wheels

H engine

J cockpit

39 Hydrogen cars are roomier than today's cars because

A they are controlled electronically

B they have small skateboard wheels

C they produce water as a byproduct

D they have an internal combustion engine

40 The main idea in the fourth paragraph of the passage is that

F hydrogen cars are becoming very popular

G funding for research on hydrogen cars is needed

H hydrogen cars will not be common for some time

J national leaders have not supported the switch to hydrogen cars

41 How do hydrogen fuel cells generate power?

A They burn gasoline.

B They burn hydrogen gas.

C They split hydrogen atoms.

D They split carbon dioxide atoms.

42 The author's likely purpose in writing this passage was to

F summarize the latest research on hydrogen cars

G explain some of the benefits of hydrogen-fueled cars

H warn people about the destruction of the environment

J explain how using hydrogen power could transform society

43 Which of these facts supports the idea that hydrogen-powered cars are environmentally friendly?

A Hydrogen-powered cars lack a steering wheel.

B Hydrogen-powered cars have a special chassis.

C Hydrogen fuel cells produce only water and heat.

D Hydrogen-powered cars convert hydrogen gas to electricity.

44 Which of these statements about hydrogen-powered cars is supported by information in the passage?

F They have a bulky engine.

G They produce harmful byproducts.

H They use a fuel made from natural gas.

J They are no faster than skateboards.

Study this library catalog card. Then answer numbers 45 through 47 by circling the letter of the best answer.

AMERICA—DISCOVERY AND EXPLORATION

973.2 **Nash, Gary B.**
N 249   Red, White and Black: the peoples of Early North
America / Gary B. Nash.—Englewood Cliffs, J.J.: Prentice-Hall,
1992. ix, 340 p. : ill., maps ; 23 cm. Includes bibliographical
references and index.

1. United States—History—Colonial period, ca. 1600–1775
2. America—Discovery and exploration
3. United States—Race Relations
4. I. Nash, Gary B. II. Title

45   According to the card, which of these sentences is true?

A The book was published in 1775.

B The book includes 340 illustrations.

C DISCOVERY AND EXPLORATION is the book's title.

D The book's subject is the peoples of early North America.

46   The numeral 973.2 refers to the classification of

F books by Gary Nash

G books containing maps

H books about American history

J books about U.S. history between 1600 and 1775

47   Which guide letters indicate the card catalog drawer in which this card would be filed?

A Rad—Rus

B Uni—Win

C Nab—Nau

D Ama—Ana

Numbers 48 through 50 are related to using reference sources. Read each item. Then choose the best answer.

48   Which of the following report topics is the most specific?

F the history of South Africa

G the South African political system

H the natural resources of Africa

J the economics of African countries

49   You can find out a country's location in relation to other countries in

A a thesaurus

B a world atlas

C a current almanac

D an unabridged dictionary

50   Most libraries shelve nonfiction books

F in alphabetical order by subject

G in numerical order by call number

H in alphabetical order by title

J in numerical order by the publisher's code number

The Language Performance Assessment is identical to the actual TABE in format and length. It will give you an idea of what the real test is like. Allow yourself 39 minutes to complete this assessment. Check your answers on pages 74–76.

Sample A

A Ashley gave I her favorite drawing.

B The children brought their portfolios home next week.

C Looking through all the interesting assignments they accomplished this year.

D We are writing our papers today.

Sample B

F Jan loves the theater did you go to the show with her last week?

G No one can believe the Annunzios got another dog?

H Why don't you put in an application at Ottawa Leather

J Today is Tuesday, August 7, 2003.

Sample C

Max buys clothes whenever he can.

His closet is stuffed with clothes.

A Max buys clothes and stuffs them into his closet.

B Because Max buys clothes whenever he can, his closet is stuffed.

C Because Max buys clothes, he likes to stuff them into his closet.

D Max buys lots of clothes so he can stuff them into his closet.

Sample D

Have you seen the school menu for the week, it doesn't look good.

F week? it

G week. It

H week? It

J week! it

For numbers 1 through 3, circle the answer that shows which punctuation mark, if any, is needed in the sentence.

1   Berne Gallery has paintings by Matisse, Picasso, Van Gogh, and Cezanne.

     A ?   **B** ,   **C** .   **D** None

2   "Why don't you get a cable Internet connection" asked Claudio.

     F ,   **G** .   **H** ?   **J** None

3   "Watch out" Brittney yelled. "Your car is rolling backward!"

     A !   **B** ,   **C** .   **D** None

For numbers 4 through 13, choose the sentence that is complete and written correctly and shows the correct capitalization and punctuation.

4   **F**   Please take those notebooks over here and put them on the conference table.

    G   Don always brings me exactly what I need for every meeting.

    H   He already took the markers in the small box to me.

    J   Please take that report to me tomorrow.

5   **A**   Keegan demonstrated "how to chop onions without crying."

    B   "Well, Zoe remarked doubtfully, "I'll give that technique a try."

    C   She asked, "Cold water or hot?" as she held the onion under the faucet.

    D   Either temperature works," Keegan answered. "But cold is best," he added.

6   **F**   He brought some groceries in the sack from the Chinese market.

    G   People who eat vegetables often are healthier than people who don't.

    H   Chop all the bite-size vegetables into pieces and mix with cooked rice.

    J   If people knew how to cook them properly, they would use Chinese vegetables more often.

7   **A**   The table is set and nearly everything else are ready for Sunday dinner.

    B   If we have enough time, let's clean the pots and pans before we eats.

    C   One of my favorite things about Sundays is leisurely dinners.

    D   The rest of the week are so rushed and frantic.

8   **F**   Some easy ways to exercise are climbing stairs, walking, and if you take care of small children.

    G   People who are motivated find the place, time, and they have the energy to exercise.

    H   If you live in a high rise, park far from the building and use the stairs.

    J   Toddlers keep you trotting, lifting, and you have to bend constantly.

9   **A**   Has everyone seen that great new movie *Welcome to the dollhouse*?

    B   Suzie read a glowing review in *Cinema Digest* a week ago tuesday.

    C   She's busy studying for her Bar Exams, but she couldn't resist.

    D   Suzie went to a matinee at Cinema One, which is up the block.

10
  F The chair of the commission asked the vice chair whether she could head the meeting.

  G Since her daughter was ill, he couldn't attend this month's meeting.

  H Kate likes to run meetings, so they was glad to take over.

  J She asked the commission members for her help, though.

11
  A Hannah Harrison's favorite book is *Tuck Everlasting*.

  B *Tuck Everlasting* is on most Book Critics' best children's book lists.

  C In december a few years ago, a movie version of *Tuck everlasting* was released.

  D Another recent movie version of a children's Novel was *The Secret Garden*.

12
  F Putting together easy-to-assemble furniture isn't always simple: however, we are going to try assemble a garden bench.

  G Reading the directions can be confusing: be sure to look at the illustrations very carefully.

  H Everyone gets a little nervous when they begin an assembly project; however, there are simple tactics you can use to make the job easier to tackle.

  J Tell yourself you can do it; thus, you'll be finished in no time!

13
  A Do you know of a good Internist at the Gerryville Clinic?

  B Freddi works as a medical photographer at Klein hospital.

  C Klein hospital is at the corner of Broad and Main in grand Rapids.

  D We'll see the hospital when we visit Grand Rapids on winter break in January.

For numbers 14 through 16, circle the word or phrase that best completes the sentence.

14 So many of the parts _____, Acme switched to a new supplier.

  F is damaged

  G are damaged

  H was damaged

  J were damaged

15 The small greyhound ran the _____ of all the pups at the dog park.

  A more fast

  B most fast

  C fastest

  D faster

16 Tyler _____ about his grandfather's accident when he started to cry.

  F talks

  G talked

  H is talking

  J was talking

For numbers 17 and 18, read the paragraph. Then choose the sentence that does not belong in the paragraph.

17 1. In recent years, coyotes have been sighted in city parks. 2. There could be several reasons for this, the main one being that the natural habitats for coyotes have continued to disappear as suburban areas take over the countryside. 3. Coyotes are predators and opportunists that have adapted well to a diet of city rodents and garbage. 4. Some people confuse coyotes with small wolves, but it's easy to tell the difference.

   A Sentence 1

   B Sentence 2

   C Sentence 3

   D Sentence 4

18 1. Their fans regard wooden roller coasters as an authentic American art form. 2. Wooden roller coaster fans travel all over the country to visit their favorite roller coasters. 3. Some people are petrified of heights and plunges and wouldn't consider riding on a roller coaster. 4. Roller coaster aficionados have compiled lists of the ten best wooden roller coasters in the United States.

   F Sentence 1

   G Sentence 2

   H Sentence 3

   J Sentence 4

For numbers 19 and 20, choose the answer that best develops the topic sentence.

19 Frank Lloyd Wright was probably the most influential architect of the twentieth century.

    A Wright believed that "form and function should be one, joined in spiritual union."

    B Born in 1867 in Richland, Wisconsin, Wright's architectural career lasted three-quarters of a century.

    C Wright created the Prairie and Usonian housing styles, which continue to influence architects today.

    D Wright built about 50 prairie-style houses in the Midwest in the decade from 1900 to 1910.

20 Gardeners use the deep winter months to plan their gardens.

    F People plant bulbs in the fall and the spring so that they can enjoy flowers in the next growing season.

    G They study plant and seed catalogues, read gardening books, and draw garden diagrams.

    H Some gardeners take classes and do lots of reading, while other gardeners rely on trial and error.

    J Water features have become increasingly popular in gardens over the last few years.

For numbers 21 through 24, read the underlined sentences. Then choose the sentence that best combines those sentences into one.

21   Dan has a terrible serve.

Dan likes to play tennis.

  A   Dan has a terrible serve, yet he likes to play tennis.

  B   Dan has a terrible serve, and he likes to play tennis.

  C   Dan has a terrible serve because he likes to play tennis.

  D   Because Dan has such a terrible serve, he likes to play tennis anyway.

22   Some motorcycle riders never wear a helmet.

Some motorcycle riders wear a helmet in city traffic or on highways.

  F   Some motorcycle riders never wear a helmet in city traffic or on highways.

  G   Some motorcycle riders never wear a helmet, while others wear a helmet in city traffic or on highways.

  H   Some motorcycle riders never wear a helmet, so others wear a helmet in city traffic or on highways.

  J   Some motorcycle riders never wear a helmet in city traffic, and others never wear a helmet on highways.

23   The President is a strong, compassionate leader.

Almost everyone who meets him admires him.

  A   An admirable leader, almost everyone who meets the President is strong and compassionate.

  B   The President is strong and compassionate, and almost everyone who meets him is admirable.

  C   Almost every admirable person who meets the President thinks he is strong and compassionate.

  D   The President is a strong, compassionate leader, admired by almost everyone who meets him.

24   Many ethical decisions are easy to make.

Others are much more difficult to resolve.

  F   Ethical decisions can be easy for some people and difficult for others.

  G   Some decisions are easier to make ethically than other decisions are to resolve.

  H   Many ethical decisions are easy to make, but others are much more difficult to resolve.

  J   Many ethical decisions are easy to make, therefore others are much more difficult to resolve.

For numbers 25 through 30, read the paragraph. Then choose the sentence that best fills the blank in the paragraph.

25 A typical yoga session often begins with a moment of centering in which participants leave everyday preoccupations behind and concentrate on the moment. Then the group may engage in breathing exercises. _____. After that, they increase the flexibility of their bodies and minds in a series of exercises called sun salutes. Floor work may follow. Nearly every yoga session ends with meditation.

    A Before they begin doing yoga, most people sit quietly for a few moments.

    B The last part of a yoga session involves cooling down and waking up.

    C The first thing yoga participants should do is dress properly in loose-fitting, comfortable clothes.

    D Next, participants do a series of simple stretches to warm up the body.

26 _____. After studying ballet in Los Angeles, she joined the Ballet Russe de Monte Carlo. Tallchief gained worldwide acclaim as prima ballerina of the New York City Ballet, where George Balanchine, her husband for several years, choreographed many roles for her, including "Firebird" to the Stravinsky score. She went on to become a celebrated ballet teacher, as well as founder of the Chicago City Ballet.

    F Of Osage Indian descent, Maria Tallchief became one of the most celebrated prima ballerinas of all time.

    G Maria Tallchief continued her career in Chicago, where she remarried and had a daughter.

    H Maria Tallchief has received many honors during her life including a Kennedy Center Honor for Lifetime Achievement.

    J Born on an Indian reservation in Fairfax, Oklahoma, Maria Tallchief displayed a talent for music at an early age.

27 The most effective way to find out whether banks discriminate in their mortgage loan practices against people of color is to use testers. The testers are typically two couples, one African-American (or another minority) and the other white, who apply for a mortgage loan at the same bank. The backgrounds and financial resources of the two couples are nearly identical. _____.

    A Nevertheless, differences in their ability to secure a mortgage can only stem from their race.

    B For example, differences in their ability to secure a mortgage can only stem from their race.

    C Therefore, differences in their ability to secure a mortgage can only stem from their race.

    D Differences in their ability to secure a mortgage, however, can only stem from their race.

28 _____. You can mix various colors of polymer clay to make new shades. You can treat the surface in many ways: by sanding; painting; buffing; or mixing in grit, ground pastels, spices—nearly any substance imaginable. Polymer clay can be molded, glued, and baked repeatedly. It can be filed, incised, shredded, draped around an armature, and rolled as thin as thread. In any crafts magazine, you're likely to learn of new possibilities for this amazing material.

F One of the newer art materials, polymer clay has been on the market for several decades.

G Polymer clay comes in a rainbow of fabulous colors.

H Polymer clay is one of the most versatile materials available to artists and craftspeople.

J There are several brands of polymer clay, each with slightly different characteristics.

29 The first Olympic games were held in 776 BC at the Greek sanctuary in Olympia. The games were part of a religious festival in honor of Zeus, the father of the gods. Koroibos, a cook from the nearby town of Elis, won the first and only event, a 600-foot-long foot race. For the next 12 centuries, the games were held at Olympia every four years. _____.

A However, by the fifth century AD, several new events had been added, including boxing, wrestling, discus, and long jump.

B Therefore, by the fifth century AD several new events had been added, including boxing, wrestling, discus, and long jump.

C Likewise several new events, including boxing, wrestling, discus, and long jump, had been added by the fifth century AD.

D Because of this tradition, by the fifth century AD several new events had been added, including boxing, wrestling, discus, and long jump.

30 On a Sunday afternoon in August 1978, an earthquake started southwest of Santa Barbara, California. The most intense motion happened in an area that includes the University of California at Santa Barbara. About 400,000 books at the UCSB library crashed to the floor. Goods flew off store shelves, windows shattered, the airport terminal tilted, mobile homes were knocked off their supports, and a landslide blocked the San Marcos Pass. Ten minutes later, a kink in the tracks made a train derail. _____.

F Before the earthquake, people's pets disappeared from sight.

G After that, people felt the earth begin to shake under their feet, and they knew an earthquake was beginning.

H During the earthquake, most people remained calm because they were used to earthquakes happening.

J After it was all over, 65 injured people went to the hospital, but no one was killed.

For numbers 31 through 37, read the letter and look at the numbered, underlined portions. Choose the answer that is written correctly for each underlined portion.

---

(31)   October, 25, 2003

(32)   Banner Displays
       102 Market Street,
       Santa Cruz, CA 99060

(33)   Dear Ms. Pinella

(34)   I feel I would be remiss if I did not never thank you for our pleasant interview and
       reiterate my interest in the position of lead designer at Banner Displays. I enjoyed our
(35)   discussion. In my excitement, however I forgot to leave my reference list, which is
       enclosed again, thanks for speaking with me.

(36)   very truly yours,
                                                                            Luz Nuncio
                                                                            Luz Nuncio

---

31
- **A** October 25 2003
- **B** October, 25 2003
- **C** October 25, 2003
- **D** Correct as it is

32
- **F** 102 Market Street
- **G** 102 Market, Street
- **H** 102 Market, Street,
- **J** Correct as it is

33
- **A** Dear Ms. Pinella;
- **B** Dear ms. Pinella,
- **C** Dear Ms. Pinella:
- **D** Correct as it is

34
- **F** did not thank you never
- **G** don't never thank you
- **H** did not thank you
- **J** Correct as it is

35
- **A** excitement however
- **B** excitement however,
- **C** excitement, however,
- **D** Correct as it is

36
- **F** enclosed again thanks
- **G** enclosed, again, thanks
- **H** enclosed. Again, thanks
- **J** Correct as it is

37
- **A** very truly yours
- **B** Very truly yours,
- **C** Very Truly yours,
- **D** Correct as it is

Page 57

Go On ▶

For numbers 38 through 42, read the paragraph and look at the numbered, underlined portions. Choose the answer that is written correctly for each underlined portion.

(38)   Grand Haven, a West Michigan town on the shore of Lake <u>Michigan is</u> a
(39) popular vacation destination. There's <u>no better place nowhere nearby</u> for
(40) families with young children. Most visitors spend <u>many happily hours</u> on the
(41) beach. Kids love the trolleys and musical <u>fountain; adults</u> like the excellent
(42) restaurants. Whatever your age, if you visit Grand Haven, you'll enjoy <u>them</u>.

38   **F** Michigan: is
       G Michigan, is
       H Michigan; is
       J Correct as it is

39   **A** no better place anywhere nearby
       B a better place nowhere nearby
       C a better place nearby
       D Correct as it is

40   **F** many happy hours
       G many happier hours
       H many more happily hours
       J Correct as it is

41   **A** fountain. adults
       B fountain, adults
       C fountain: adults
       D Correct as it is

42   **F** it
       G that
       H those
       J Correct as it is

For numbers 43 through 46, read the paragraph and look at the numbered, underlined portions. Choose the answer that is written correctly for each underlined portion.

(43)   Abyssinian cats are elegant, intelligent, and <u>people love them</u>. They are one

(44)   of the oldest breeds, though <u>no one doesn't know</u> exactly how old. Abyssinian

(45)   cats have long-limbed, <u>muscularly</u> bodies, arched necks, and large ears.

They have been popular at cat shows for more than a century, and people

(46)   <u>will always be interested</u> in these beautiful animals.

43   **A** lovely

        B lovable

        C love people

        D Correct as it is

44   **F** one does know

        G no one knows

        H one doesn't know

        J Correct as it is

45   **A** muscley

        B muscular

        C more muscled

        D Correct as it is

46   **F** will always have been interested

        G is always interested

        H were always interested

        J Correct as it is

For numbers 47 through 50, read the paragraph and look at the numbered, underlined portions. Choose the answer that is written correctly for each underlined portion.

(47)   *Dancing in starlight* won the film critic's special award for first-time

(48)   directors at this year's new York Film Festival. The competition for the coveted

(49)   award was especially fiercely this year because there were many outstanding

(50)   entries. To quote judge Herman Miller, "Gosh I just closed my eyes and voted

         for the first film that came to mind."

47   **A** *Dancing In Starlight*
          B *Dancing in Starlight*
          C *dancing in starlight*
          D Correct as it is

48   **F** new york film festival
          G New york film festival
          H New York Film Festival
          J Correct as it is

49   **A** fierce
          B fiercer
          C more fierce
          D Correct as it is

50   **F** Gosh.
          G Gosh:
          H Gosh,
          J Correct as it is

For numbers 51 through 55, read the paragraph and look at the numbered, underlined portions. Choose the answer that is written correctly for each underlined portion.

(51)   What's the <u>difference or distinction</u> between a recession and a depression? There's an old joke that says it's a recession when your neighbor loses his job

(52)   and a depression when you lose your job. After all, your <u>neighbors</u> job isn't as

(53)   important to you as your own job! Both are <u>extended declines in business activity</u>.

(54)   A depression lasts <u>longer. And</u> displays a larger decline in economic activity than

(55)   a recession does. During a recession, companies reduce <u>their</u> workforce and consumers have less money to spend.

51   **A** difference

      B difference and distinction

      C difference or the distinction

      D Correct as it is

52   **F** neighbor's

      G neighbors'

      H neighbors's

      J Correct as it is

53   **A** business activity extended declines

      B extended business activity in decline

      C in extended decline business activity

      D Correct as it is

54   **F** longer and

      G longer, and

      H longer; And

      J Correct as it is

55   **A** his

      B its

      C her

      D Correct as it is

STOP

The Spelling Performance Assessment is identical to the actual TABE in format and length. It will give you an idea of what the real test is like. Allow yourself 10 minutes to complete this assessment. Check your answers on page 76.

Sample A

Mary enjoys wild _____.

A whether

B wether

C weather

D wetter

For numbers 1 through 20, choose the word that is spelled correctly and best completes the sentence.

1   I understand what you mean when you say "_____ is bliss."

A Ignorrance

B Ignourance

C Ignorance

D Ignoreance

2   Jurors should be _____ when they decide a case.

F impartial

G imparshul

H imparshial

J impartiale

3   I received my college _____ letter.

A acceptanse

B acceptunce

C acceptance

D acceptence

4   Your answer is a _____ answer.

F valod

G valed

H valud

J valid

5 I should have _____ to the top-secret files.

   A accuss

   B access

   C acess

   D acces

6 Amber always accepts the _____ assignments.

   F playrite

   G playright

   H playwrite

   J playwright

7 Being a professional musician is my greatest _____.

   A aspiration

   B aspuration

   C aspuhration

   D asperation

8 Did he _____ what kind of ice cream he wants?

   F spessifie

   G spescify

   H specify

   J spessify

9 I have never been accused of being _____.

   A scrupuluss

   B scrupules

   C scrupulus

   D scrupulous

10 Maria is a _____ snowboarder.

   F novise

   G noviss

   H novice

   J novisce

11 Be _____ about your record-keeping.

   A systimatic

   B systamatic

   C systematic

   D systumatic

12 Understanding math is key to understanding _____.

   F stitistics

   G stetistics

   H stutistics

   J statistics

Performance Assessment: Spelling

13 There is no _____ for a decision like this.

    A precedent

    B precedint

    C precedant

    D precedunt

14 For as long as he can remember, Ed has wanted to be an _____.

    F ambassadir

    G ambassader

    H ambassador

    J ambassadur

15 They've already released a _____ to the new blockbuster movie.

    A sequell

    B sequal

    C sequel

    D sequil

16 We're out of eggs and bacon, so cereal and fruit will have to _____.

    F sufice

    G suffice

    H suffise

    J suffisce

17 The referee had to _____ in the middle of a play.

    A interveine

    B interveane

    C intervene

    D interveene

18 Caitlin works in the _____ department.

    F personell

    G personnell

    H personel

    J personnel

19 Math and science are _____ courses.

    A compoulsory

    B compalsory

    C compulsory

    D compuhlsory

20 The perennials have been _____ since winter set in.

    F dormant

    G dormint

    H dormunt

    J dormont

STOP ✳

Practice 1 (pages 8–9)

1. **D** *The Reader's Guide to Periodical Literature* lists articles in magazines by topic. Option A is incorrect because this source lists books. Option B is a word reference. Option C is a collection of informational articles on many subjects.

2. **H** Fiction books are shelved from A to Z by the author's last name, since these books do not have specific subjects. Option F is incorrect because fiction books do not have call numbers, which refer to subject areas. Option G is incorrect because publication dates do not clearly distinguish one book from another. Books are not arranged by title (option J).

3. **B** World almanacs contain many facts about recent events. Option A is incorrect because an almanac is not a word reference. Option C is incorrect because almanacs emphasize facts, not maps. Option D is incorrect because almanacs do not feature history articles.

4. **G** A thesaurus allows you to find words with similar meanings. Option F is a map reference. Option H is a word reference. Option J is a part of a book containing supplementary information.

5. **A** The publication date is given in line 4 on the card. Option B is one of the subjects of the book, which is listed at the bottom of the card. Option C is the number of pages, not illustrations. Option D is incorrect because the author's name is Thomas Christopher.

6. **G** The call number refers to the main subject area, which is listed first in the list of subjects at the bottom of the card. Option F is too broad. Option H does not fit the subject of the book. Option J is too specific to be an overall subject classification.

7. **B** The form does not ask for the date of the illness or injury. Box 2 asks for the name of the patient (option A). Box 1 asks for the carrier's name and address (option C). Box 3 asks for the health insurance claim number (option D).

8. **H** Roberto should write the claim number in Box 3. Option F is not correct because Box 1 is for the carrier's name and address. Option G is not correct because Box 2 is for the name of the patient. Option J is not correct because Box 4 is where Roberto should write the date of the claim denial.

9. **B** Option B best summarizes Roberto's injury, so it is the best answer. Option A is not correct because it does not completely describe the injury. It does not include that it occurred while Roberto was jogging. Options C and D are not correct because they do not describe the injury.

10. **H** Roberto has a letter from his doctor to submit, so he should check "I have additional evidence to submit" in Box 7. Option F is not correct because Roberto does have evidence. Option G is not correct because

"Attach such evidence to this form" is a direction line within Box 7; it is not an option in Box 7. Option J is not correct because it is not an option in Box 7.

Practice 2 (page 11)

1. **B** The second paragraph clarifies that people with a *sedentary* lifestyle "are not active at all." The opposite of "not active" is *active.* Option A is incorrect because *lazy* is similar in meaning to *sedentary.* Options C and D are incorrect because *unhealthy* and *thoughtful* are not opposites of *sedentary.*

2. **G** The passage gives "brisk walking or bicycling," both very energetic activities, as examples of *vigorous* activities. Option F does not fit because these activities may or may not be difficult. Option H is incorrect because these activities are not moderate activities. Option J is incorrect because these activities are not necessarily dangerous.

3. **D** The passage explains that clots "can *block* the flow of blood." Option A is incorrect because cells by definition do not block something. Option C is incorrect because networks connect rather than block things. Option B is incorrect because spaces are openings that let things through, not block things.

4. **J** In paragraph four, the phrase "these substances" refers to "compounds" in the previous sentence. Thus, *substances* and *compounds* are synonyms. Options F (gases) and H (liquids) are not correct because they do not have the same meaning as *compound.* Option G refers to a different meaning of *compound* that does not fit the health context of the passage.

5. **D** Since the risks of heart disease are something that a person would want to reduce, "guard against" makes the most sense as the meaning of "fend off." Also, the word "reduce" is used in a similar sentence at the beginning of the paragraph. Options A and B are incorrect because they express a positive attitude toward risk. Option C is incorrect because the passage suggests that foods can help to reduce the chance of disease, but not eliminate it altogether.

6. **G** The paragraph is about how foods can promote a healthy heart; the word "nutritious" describes these foods, so they too are "healthy." The opposite of healthy is "unhealthy." Options F, H, and J are incorrect because tasty foods, uncooked foods, or low-calorie foods may or may not be nutritious.

Practice 3 (page 13)

1. **B** Paragraph three explains that digging furrows is a way to halt a forest fire, and shovels are listed as one tool for digging. Option A is incorrect because the

passage does not mention lasers. Option C is incorrect because paragraph three implies that bulldozers are used infrequently. Option D is incorrect because water hoses are not mentioned and would seldom be used in remote locations.

2. **F** In the second and third paragraphs, spotting a fire (option G) is mentioned first, then determining its direction (option H), developing a strategy (option J), and finally building a fire break. Therefore, option F is the correct answer.

3. **C** The fourth paragraph discusses the dangers posed by changing wind direction. Options A, B, and D are incorrect because the passage does not describe any dangers to firefighters posed by campfires, traveling by helicopter, or hiking over rough terrain.

4. **G** The second paragraph states that most surveillance, or spotting, "is done by airplane or helicopter." The passage does not mention fire spotting by satellite (option F) or by campers and backpackers (option H), so these choices are incorrect. Option J is incorrect because most fire spotting is done by air, while towers are located on the ground.

5. **B** Paragraph one states that most wildfires "are caused by human carelessness," so option B is correct. For option A, drought is a contributing factor, but not the main factor, in causing forest fires. For option C, smokers cause ten percent, not most, forest fires. Option D is incorrect because the first paragraph states that only a small number of fires are caused by lightning.

6. **J** The second paragraph describes communication through two-way radios, and the last paragraph states that "good communication" is "critical" for stopping a fire. Option F is incorrect because wind works against the firefighters. Option G is incorrect because the passage discusses building firebreaks rather than dropping water, as the main way to fight fires. Option H is incorrect because a "can-do" attitude is not mentioned in the passage.

Practice 4 (page 15)

1. **D** The fifth paragraph explains that students who used racial insults were taken to the principal's office. The passage doesn't say that racial insults led to private English lessons (option A), a visit to Miss Ryan's class (option B), or a wrestling match with Manual (option C).

2. **J** The passage is about Ernesto's experience at Lincoln, so option J is the correct answer. Options F, G, and H are not correct because they are details from the passage, not the main idea of the passage.

3. **D** Ernesto can be described as sensitive because he had feelings of love for his teacher. It is also a fact that he graduated from first grade with honors. Therefore, option D is the best answer. Options A, B, and C are not correct because they include details that may be true, but are not specifically supported by the passage.

4. **H** The passage says that Ernesto had friends and neighbors of many different nationalities. Option F is not correct because it implies that there was racial intolerance. A trip to the principal's office is only necessary when there is racial intolerance. Option G is not correct because it also implies that there was racial intolerance. Option J is not correct because the fact that the town is racially mixed does not show that living in a racially mixed neighborhood promotes racial tolerance.

5. **C** Miss Ryan was Ernesto's English teacher, and he said that it was as if they "were both discovering together the secrets of the English language." Therefore, option C is correct. Option A is not correct because Miss Hopley was the principal, not an English teacher. Although Ernesto may have learned some English from his classmates (option B) and his family (option D), the passage does not support these options.

6. **G** Option G is correct because the passage describes Miss Ryan's gentle and patient nature. Options F, H, and J are not correct because they are not supported by information in the passage.

Practice 5 (page 17)

1. **B** An opinion is a statement that involves a judgment. Only option B fits this definition. Options A, C, and D are facts that are stated or can be inferred from the excerpt.

2. **F** The author is saying that Frankie was acting strangely. Option G is not correct because the story does not say that Frankie had a sunburn. Options H and J are not correct because Frankie's loneliness and suffering does not come up until later in the story.

3. **B** Option B is correct based on John Henry's statement, "They hauled her out of the wedding car." Options A and D are incorrect because the excerpts do not mention a gift or how Frankie's dress looked. Option C is incorrect based on John Henry's statement above.

4. **F** Frankie says, "Not to belong to a 'we' makes you too lonesome." Options G and H are incorrect because she does not show any feelings of superiority or anger toward others. Option J is incorrect because thinking about being a "we" makes Frankie feel positive, or optimistic, not pessimistic.

5. **B** Frankie is feeling lonely and struggling to accept an uncomfortable fact in her life. Readers can easily identify with these feelings and may remember similar emotions when they were young. Also, the concerned responses of other characters such as Berenice, who listens and comforts Frankie, and Janice, who tries to reassure her, help the reader to empathize with Frankie. Options A and C are incorrect because the main emphasis in the excerpts is on Frankie's unhappiness and disappointment. Option D is incorrect because Frankie's feelings of

uncertainty and loneliness are not unusual in young adolescents.

6. **H** Frankie's desire to be close to someone else is very strong, even though it was not right in the case of Janice and Jarvis. Option F is unlikely because Berenice continues to support Frankie with positive suggestions and frankness. Option G is not likely because Frankie now realizes that living with Janice and Jarvis is impossible. Option J is unlikely because Frankie is older than John Henry.

7. **D** Frankie's desperate statements communicate her misery. Options A, B, and C do not fit because Frankie does not show any signs of feeling happy, nervous, or resigned.

8. **G** The excerpts highlight the fact that Frankie is growing up and on the brink of adulthood. She still enjoys some childish things, like playing with John Henry, but is fascinated by the adult idea of married love. Her struggle to accept her separateness and her desire for love and acceptance are common when growing up. Options F and H are incorrect because neither love nor helping others is the main focus in the excerpts. Option J is incorrect because the characters' speeches in the excerpts do not address discovering one's talents.

Practice 6 (pages 18–19)

1. **B** *Was* is correct because the singular subject *Ida B. Wells* requires a past tense singular verb. Option A is incorrect because *is* is in the present tense. Options C and D are plural. [Subject/Verb Agreement]

2. **G** *Her* is correct because the sentence requires an object pronoun that takes the place of *Ida B. Wells*. Option F is incorrect because *me* can not take the place of *Ida B. Wells*. Option H is incorrect because it shows ownership. Option J is incorrect because *she* is not an object pronoun. [Objective Pronoun]

3. **A** The past tense verb *died* is required because the action in the sentence happened in the past. Options B, C, and D are incorrect because they are not in the past tense. [Past Tense]

4. **F** *Better* is correct because the sentence needs a comparative adjective to compare Wells to most other teachers. Options G, H, and J are incorrect because they are not correctly formed comparative adjectives. [Comparative Adjective]

5. **C** *Alarmingly* is correct because an adverb is required in this sentence to modify the verb *increased*. Options A, B, and D do not correctly modify *increased*. [Choose Between Adjective and Adverb]

6. **H** *Her* is correct because a possessive feminine pronoun is needed in the sentence. Options F and J are not possessive. Option G is masculine. [Possessive Pronoun]

7. **A** *Are* is correct because the plural subject *African Americans* requires a present tense plural verb. Options B and C are not in the present tense. Option D is incorrect because *is* is singular. [Subject and Verb Agreement]

8. **J** *Will admire* is correct because it is in the future tense. Options F, G, and H are incorrect because they are not in the future tense. [Future Tense]

9. **D** The phrase *over the years* denotes actions that began in the past and are ongoing. Therefore the perfect tense *have written* is correct. Option A is in the present tense. Option B is in the future tense. Option C needs a helping verb. [Perfect Tense]

10. **G** The phrase *when she started an African American newspaper* implies that Wells was doing something else when she started the newspaper. Therefore, *was teaching* is correct because it indicates what she was doing and it is a continuing past action. Option F is incorrect because it is in the present tense. Option H is incorrect because it is in the future tense. Option J is incorrect because it is in the perfect tense. [Progressive Tense]

11. **D** All issues are being compared, so the superlative adverb is the correct choice. Option A is not a word. Option B does not make a comparison. Option C compares just two things. [Superlative Adverb]

12. **H** The sentence uses *borrow* correctly. We *borrow* things from others. Other people *lend* things to us. Options F and G use *borrow* and *lend* incorrectly. Option J is incorrect because the verb *sit* should be *set*. [Easily Confused Verbs]

13. **D** The sentence is correct because it has one negative word—*no*. Option A has *never* and *no one*, option B has *hadn't* and *not*, and option C has *wasn't*, *scarcely*, and *never*. [Use Negative]

14. **F** The sentence uses the correct superlative form *most heroic*. Option G is the form used to compare only two items. Option H is incorrect because *hero* is not an adjective. Option J is incorrect because *heroicest* is an incorrect superlative form. [Superlative Adjective]

15. **A** Option A is correct because a comparative adjective is required in this sentence. Option B uses a superlative adjective, which compares more than two things. Options C and D are not correct because they are not adjectives. [Comparative Adjective]

16. **J** The pronoun *she* agrees with its antecedent *Wells*. In option F, the singular noun *friend* does not agree with the plural pronoun *their*. In option G, *he* should be *they*. In option H, *he* should be *they*. [Antecedent Agreement]

Practice 7 (pages 20–21)

1. **C** The sentences require *which* to introduce the dependent clause. Option A lacks a conjunction. Options B and D imply cause, which is not indicated in the sentences. [Sentence Combining: Coordinating]

2. **H** The sentences require a coordinating conjunction to combine them. *So* is the coordinating conjunction that makes sense, so option H is correct. Option F lacks a conjunction. The coordinating conjunctions *and* and *for* in Options G and J do not make sense

when used to combine the two sentences. [Sentence Combining: Subordinating]

3. **C** Modifiers should accompany the words they modify as closely as possible, so the adverb *fluently* should follow the verb *wrote*. Therefore, option C is correct. Option A is incorrect because it changes the adverb to an adjective. Options B and D are incorrect because they place the adverb in the wrong position. [Sentence Combining: Adding Modifier]

4. **H** Option H is correct because it does not repeat words that have nearly the same meaning. The words *rush out* and *hurry* mean the same thing. Options F, G, and J include repetitive words and phrases. [Verbosity and Repetition]

5. **A** Option A is correct because it correctly divides the words into two sentences. Options B, C, and D are run-on sentences. [Sentence Recognition: Complete and Fragment and Run-On]

6. **F** Option F is correct because it creates a parallel structure. *Consult* and *search* are both in the same verb form. Options G, H, and J create nonparallel structures. [Nonparallel Structure]

7. **B** Option B is correct because *full of tools* clearly refers to the chest. Options A, C, and D are incorrect because they have misplaced modifiers that create ambiguous meanings. [Misplaced Modifier]

8. **H** Option H is correct because it does not repeat words with similar meanings. Options F, G, and J are incorrect because each repeats words with nearly identical meanings. [Verbosity and Repetition]

9. **D** Option D is correct because it is a complete sentence. Options A, B, and C are sentence fragments. [Sentence Recognition: Complete and Fragment and Run-On]

10. **G** Option G is correct because the verbs have parallel structure. The verbs in options F, H, and J are nonparallel. [Nonparallel Structure]

11. **A** Option A is correct because the modifier is placed correctly and does not create an ambiguous meaning. Options C, D, and F are incorrect because misplaced modifiers create two possible meanings. [Misplaced Modifier]

12. **G** Option G is correct because it is a complete sentence. Options F, H, and J are run-on sentences. [Sentence Recognition: Complete and Fragment and Run-On]

Practice 8 (pages 22–23)

1. **C** Option C is correct because it expresses the main idea of the paragraph. It is the topic sentence. The rest of the sentences of the paragraph support this topic sentence. Options A, B, and D are true statements, but they are incorrect because they do not express the main point of the paragraph. [Topic Sentence]

2. **J** This sentence is correct because it supports and develops the preceding sentence. Option F places Kahlo's death too early in the sequence of events. Options G and H give details about Rivera too early

in the sequence of events, before Rivera is introduced. [Sequence]

3. **A** This sentence is correct because it contains the transition word *Surely.* The sentence makes sense as a conclusion to the paragraph. Options B, C, and D are incorrect because these sentences and their transition words do not make sense as conclusions to the paragraph. [Connective and Transition]

4. **H** This sentence is not related to the topic of making pasta. Options F, G, and J are correct because they all relate directly to the main idea. [Unrelated Sentence]

5. **C** Option C is not related to the topic of giving a party. Options A, B, and D all relate directly to the topic. [Unrelated Sentence]

6. **H** This sentence is correct because it develops and gives background details about the topic sentence. Options F, G, and J do not build on the topic sentence. [Supporting Sentences]

7. **C** This sentence develops and supports the topic sentence. Options A, B, and D do not support the topic sentence. [Supporting Sentences]

Practice 9 (pages 24–25)

1. **A** *John A. Roebling* is correct because a person's name is a proper noun. All the parts of a person's name are capitalized. Options B, C, and D are incorrect because one or more of the words is not capitalized. Option D is also incorrect because *Roebling's* is possessive. [Capitalization: Name]

2. **H** The phrase *grand suspension bridge* is describing a kind of bridge. It is not the name of the bridge. Therefore, it should not be capitalized. Options F, G, and J are incorrect because some of the words are capitalized. [Capitalization: Proper Noun]

3. **D** *Brooklyn Bridge* is the name of a bridge. Therefore, that makes it a proper noun, so all the words in the bridge's name must be capitalized. Options A, B, and C are incorrect because not all the words in the name are capitalized. [Capitalization: Geographic Name]

4. **J** The title of the book is correct as it is. Option F is incorrect because *great bridge* should be capitalized. Option G is incorrect because the second instance of *bridge* also should be capitalized. Option H is not correct because the first instance *Of The* should not be capitalized. [Capitalization: Title of Work]

5. **C** *David McCullough* is correctly capitalized. Options A, B, and D are incorrect because not all the parts of the name are capitalized. [Capitalization: Name]

6. **G** The movie title, a proper noun, is correctly capitalized. Options F and J are incorrect because people's names and titles must be capitalized. Option H is incorrect because the capitalized words are common nouns, not proper nouns. [Capitalization: Proper Noun]

7. **B** The names of the national park and the lake are proper nouns and are capitalized correctly. Option A is incorrect because *National Park*, a common

noun, is capitalized. In options C and D, the proper nouns are not capitalized correctly. [Capitalization: Proper Noun]

8. F The proper noun *Dr. Ruiz* is capitalized correctly. Options G, H, and J are incorrect because the sentences include proper nouns that are not capitalized. [Capitalization: Proper Noun]

9. C The class title is capitalized correctly. Options A and B are incorrect because they have common nouns (*Middle School* and *Summer*) that are incorrectly capitalized. Option D is incorrect because the initial *p.* is not capitalized. [Capitalization: Proper Noun]

10. F This sentence is correct because the proper noun *Scoops* is capitalized. Options G, H, and J include common nouns (*Family, Dozens, Waffle Cones*) that should not be capitalized. [Capitalization: Proper Noun]

11. D All parts of the school name, a proper noun, are correctly capitalized. Options A, B, and C are incorrect because some of the proper nouns are not capitalized. [Capitalization: Proper Noun]

12. G All parts of the school name, a proper noun, are correctly capitalized. Option F is incorrect because *Veterinarian* should not be capitalized. Option H is not correct because part of the school name is not capitalized. Option J is not correct because *gary* is not capitalized. [Capitalization: Proper Noun]

13. D *Grand Canyon* is correct because the name of a geographic place is a proper noun, and proper nouns must be capitalized. Option A is incorrect because *College Professor* is a common noun and should not be capitalized. In options B and C, the proper nouns are not capitalized correctly. [Capitalization: Geographic Name]

Practice 10 (pages 26–27)

1. B A comma is correct because commas must separate items in a series. A comma is needed after the first *mysteries*. Options A and C use the wrong punctuation marks. Option D is incorrect because items in a series require commas. [Comma]

2. D The sentence is correct as written. The question mark follows the quotation because the sentence asks the question, not the quotation. Options F, G, and H are unnecessary punctuation marks. [Question Mark]

3. A The two closely related independent clauses can be punctuated with a semicolon. Options B, C, and D are incorrect because they use the wrong punctuation mark or no punctuation mark to separate the clauses. [Semicolon]

4. F Option F is correct because a parenthetical expression must be separated from the rest of the sentence with a comma. Option G is incorrect because it uses the wrong punctuation mark. Option H is incorrect because *A* should not be capitalized when it follows a comma. Option J is incorrect because it lacks the needed comma. [Introductory Element]

5. C The sentence requires a comma after *saying* because the parenthetical expression must be set off with commas. Options A, B, and D do not set off the parenthetical expression with commas. [Commas]

6. H The sentences must be separated by a period since they are not closely related independent clauses. They are sentences and must be punctuated like sentences. Options F, G, and J use the wrong punctuation. [Semicolon]

7. D This sentence is correctly punctuated because the parenthetical expression is correctly set off with commas. Options A, B and C are not correct because they do not set off the parenthetical expression with commas. [Commas]

8. H Option H is correct because commas must separate the items in a series. Options F, G, and J do not separate all the items in a series with commas. [Commas]

9. D The sentence is correct as it is because the appositive is set off from the rest of the sentence by commas. Options A, B, and C do not set off the appositive with commas. [Commas]

10. H This sentence is correct because the items in the series are separated by commas, as they should be. Options F, G, and J are incorrect because they do not separate each item in the series with a comma. [Commas]

11. B This sentence correctly separates the parenthetical expression, *as you know*, from the rest of the sentence with a comma. Options A and D are missing the needed comma. Option C is incorrect because *Jan* should not be followed with a comma. [Commas]

12. J This sentence is correct because the items in the series are set off with commas. Options F, G, and H are incorrect because not all of the items in the series are set off with commas. [Commas]

13. C The parenthetical expression *Surprisingly* is correctly set off with a comma. Options A, B, and D do not set off the parenthetical expression with a comma. [Commas]

Practice 11 (pages 28–29)

1. B This date is punctuated correctly with a comma after the date. Options A, C, and D are incorrect because the comma is lacking or is in the wrong position. [Parts of a Letter]

2. F This address line is correct because it neither needs nor has a punctuation mark. Options G, H, and J have unnecessary punctuation marks. [Parts of a Letter]

3. D This address line is correct because it has a comma separating the city and state. Options A, B, and C either lack a comma or have incorrectly placed commas. [Parts of a Letter]

4. F This salutation is correct because it is followed by a colon. Options G, H, and J either lack punctuation or have incorrect punctuation. [Parts of a Letter]

5. B This closing is correct because it is followed by a comma. Options A, C, and D either lack punctuation or have incorrect punctuation. [Parts of a Letter]

6. J This phrase is punctuated correctly because the city and state are set off by commas, as they should be. Options F and G are incorrect because each lacks a comma. Option H is incorrect because it has a semicolon, instead of a comma. [Parts of a Letter]

7. B *Sister's* is correct because it is the singular possessive form. Option A lacks an apostrophe, which is needed to show possession. Option C is an incorrect plural form. Option D is incorrect because *sisters'* is the plural possessive form. [Apostrophe]

8. H This option uses a comma with a quotation correctly. Option F needs a comma in place of the period. Option G needs a comma in place of the semicolon. Option J lacks the necessary comma. [Quotation Marks]

9. B The quotation marks and commas are correctly placed. Option A is incorrect because the question mark should be inside the ending quotation mark. Options C and D are incorrect because the ending quotation mark is in the wrong place. [Quotation Marks]

10. G The quotation marks and exclamation point are correctly placed. Option F needs a comma between *Mall* and the ending quotation mark. Option H needs a comma in place of the period. Option J is missing the first quotation mark. [Quotation Marks]

11. C This answer is correct because the ending quotation mark is missing from the sentence. It should be placed after the question mark. Options A, B, and D call for unnecessary punctuation. [Quotation Marks]

12. J The sentence is punctuated correctly as it is. Options F, G, and H call for unnecessary punctuation. [Quotation Marks]

13. B This answer is correct because the sentence is missing end punctuation. A period should be placed after *fantasy* and before the ending quotation mark. Options A and C call for unnecessary punctuation. Option D is incorrect because the sentence needs end punctuation. [Quotation Marks]

14. J This answer is correct because the sentence is correctly punctuated. Options F, G, and H call for unnecessary punctuation. [Quotation Marks]

Practice 12 (page 30)

1. B *Statistics* is the correct spelling. The first syllable has the "uh" sound, which is spelled with an *a* in this case. Options A, C, and D are misspelled. [Schwa]

2. H *Discreet* is the correct spelling. The second syllable has the long *e* sound, which is spelled *ee* in this case. Options F, G, and J are misspelled. [Long Vowel]

3. C *Aspiration* is the correct spelling. The second syllable has the "uh" vowel sound, which is spelled with an *i* in this case. Options A, B, and D are misspelled. [Schwa]

4. F *Intervene* is the correct spelling. The last syllable is a long vowel. It sounds just like the letter *e*. Options G, H, and J are misspelled. [Long Vowel]

5. C *Valid* is the correct spelling. Options A, B, and D are misspelled. [Short Vowel]

6. F *Charitable* is the correct spelling. The third syllable has the "uh" vowel sound, which is spelled with an *a* in this case. Options G, H, and J are misspelled. [Schwa]

7. C *Systematic* is the correct spelling. Options A, B, and D are misspelled. [Short Vowel]

8. G *Brevity* is the correct spelling. Options F, H, and J are misspelled. [Long Vowel]

Practice 13 (page 31)

1. B *Specify* is the correct spelling. The *s* sound is spelled with a *c*. Options A, C, and D are misspelled. [Variant Spelling Consonants]

2. H *Impartial* is the correct spelling. The *sh* sound is spelled with a *ti*. Options F, G, and J are misspelled. [Variant Spelling Consonants]

3. B *Novice* is the correct spelling. The *s* sound is spelled with a *c*. Options A, C, and D are misspelled. [Variant Spelling Consonants]

4. J *Playwright* is the correct spelling. Options F, G, and H are misspelled. [Silent Letter Consonants]

5. C *Access* is the correct spelling. Options A, B, and D are misspelled. [Double Letter Consonants]

6. H *Personnel* is the correct spelling. Options F, G, and J are misspelled. [Double Letter Consonants]

7. D *Susceptible* is the correct spelling because the silent *c* is included. Options A, B, and C are misspelled. [Silent Letter Consonants]

8. H *Scientific* is the correct spelling because the silent *c* is included. Options F, G, and J are misspelled. [Silent Letter Consonants]

Practice 14 (page 32)

1. C *Stationery* is the correct spelling. Option A is incorrect because the homonym does not make sense in the sentence. Options B and D are misspelled. [Homonym]

2. F *Precedent* is the correct spelling. The word ending is spelled correctly. To figure out how to spell this word, think about how to spell similar words, like *accident*. Options G, H, and J are misspelled. [Similar Word Part]

3. C *Expedient* is the correct spelling. The word ending is spelled correctly. To figure out how to spell this word, think about how to spell similar words, like *ingredient* or *obedient*. Options, A, B, and D have misspelled word endings. [Similar Word Part]

4. H *Lightning* is the correct spelling. Option J is incorrect because the homonym does not make sense in the sentence. Options F and G are misspelled. [Homonym]

5. C *Acceptance* is the correct spelling. The word ending is spelled correctly. To figure out how to spell this word, think about how to spell similar words, like *distance* or *substance*. Options A, B, and D have misspelled word endings. [Similar Word Part]

6. F *Ignorance* is the correct spelling because the *e* was dropped from the root word *ignore* when the ending *–ance* was added. Options G, H, and J are misspelled. [Root]

7. D *Ambassador* is the correct spelling. The suffix is spelled correctly with an *-or*. In options A, B, and C, the suffix is misspelled. [Suffix]

8. F *Scrupulous* is the correct spelling. The suffix is spelled correctly with an *-ous*. Options G, H, and J are misspelled. [Suffix]

Performance Assessment: Reading (pages 33–48)

A. C Option C is correct because when it is dark you turn on the lights, not the oven (option A), radio (option B), or computer (option D).

B. J The paragraph clearly states that Marla left the party to help her brother, whose car had broken down. The paragraph does not say that her car had broken down (option F) or that she wasn't having a good time (option H). Her phone was working or she could not have received the call from her brother (option G).

1. B The sentence in which the word occurs refers to saving money, and spending little helps to save money. Options A, C, and D are incorrect because their meanings do not relate to saving money. [Same Meaning]

2. G Della's wish to buy Jim something fine is based on her feelings for him, not the fact that they are poor. Options F, H, and J are incorrect because the couple's shabby apartment (option F), Della's tiny savings (option H), and Jim's lack of gloves (option J) all show that they are poor. [Supporting Evidence]

3. B The nod is in response to Madame Sofronie's offer of $20 to buy Della's hair. Option A is incorrect because Della finds the right gift for Jim *after* she meets with Madame Sofronie. Option C is incorrect because Jim sees Della's hair later in the story. Option D is incorrect because nodding means acceptance, not bargaining. [Style Techniques]

4. H Both Jim and Della give up something they treasure in order to buy a gift for the other. Option F is incorrect because both gifts are costly compared to what the couple could afford. Option G is incorrect because the combs and watch chain are practical as well as beautiful. Option J is incorrect because Jim didn't know what gift Della has purchased before he buys one for her. [Character Aspects]

5. B The most important fact about Della and Jim is that each give up their most prized possession for the other, thus showing their love and generosity for one another. Options A, C, and D are incorrect because the *main* emphasis of the passage is not on Della's and Jim's foolishness (option A), how the poor can find ways to buy presents (option C), or

choosing beautiful gifts (option D). [Summary and Paraphrase]

6. H The gifts are highly valued by both characters. In addition, Della's hair will grow back, and Jim will likely earn enough money to have a watch again. Option F is incorrect because the passage emphasizes the couple's love and compatibility. Option G is incorrect because children are not mentioned in the passage. Option J is incorrect because the gifts are too important to return. [Predict Outcomes]

7. C The map shows police precincts, and each precinct has its own police station. Options A, B, and D are incorrect because the map does not show shopping areas, polling stations, or elementary schools. [Main Idea]

8. F High Street is the boundary between the two precincts and Weber Road crosses this street. Part of Weber Road is in precinct 3 and part is in precinct 2. Option G is incorrect because all of Weber Road is on one side of Alum Creek. Option H is incorrect because all of Weber Road is on one side of Morse Road. Option J is incorrect because all of Weber Road lies inside the city limits. [Maps]

9. C Bethel Road lines up with the boundary of precinct 3 in the upper left corner of the map. Option A is incorrect because Ferris Road falls within the boundaries of precinct 2. Options B and D are incorrect because Cooke Road and North Broadway do not line up with any of the boundaries of precinct 3. [Maps]

10. G The intersection of Oakland Park and McGuffy falls within the boundaries of precinct 2. Option F is incorrect because precinct 1 is not shown on the map. Option H is incorrect because neither Oakland Park nor McGuffy falls within the boundaries of precinct 3. Option J is incorrect because precinct 4 is not shown on the map. [Maps]

11. D North Broadway crosses High Street, which is a boundary between precincts 3 and 2. Option A is incorrect because Reed Road is on the edge of precinct 3, but not in precinct 2. Option B is incorrect because Joyce Avenue is in precinct 2, but not precinct 3. Option C is incorrect because Highland Drive falls in precinct 3, but not in precinct 2. [Maps]

12. H The court said race was "a plus factor" in college admissions and thus positive or important. Paying attention to race leads to a diverse campus, so this result too is "important." Options F, G, and J are incorrect because they are weaker or negative words that do not go with the idea of importance. [Same Meaning]

13. D This option refers to a quota, or set-aside. Option A is incorrect because a "plus factor" is not a quota. Options B and C are incorrect because they do not refer to quotas or to colleges. [Supporting Evidence]

14. G This option states something about the real world that can be proven. It is a fact. Options F, H, and J are incorrect because they express a point of view or value judgment that is open to dispute, as shown by the words "is the fairest" (option F), "is still a worthy goal" (option H), and "should focus on" (option J). [Fact and Opinion]

15. A The phrase "reverse discrimination" is used in the sentence that claims that qualified applicants are "bypassed" in favor of less qualified applicants. The sentence does not imply that reverse discrimination affects a specific group, making options B, C, and D incorrect. [Stated Concept]

16. J The first sentence of the last paragraph says that the Supreme Court established that numerical quotas do not treat all citizens equally. The passage does not say that the Supreme Court compared numerical quotas to reverse discrimination (option F), traditional discrimination (option G), or equal opportunity (option H). [Compare and Contrast]

17. D Paragraph 3 of the passage cites this fact in connection with Bakke's lawsuit. Options A, B, and C are incorrect because they misstate the University of California's affirmative action policy. [Supporting Evidence]

18. H The Civil Rights Act of 1964 is mentioned first in the passage, which presents events in time order. Options F, G, and J are incorrect because they all occurred after 1964. Bakke applied to the university of California in the late 1970s (option J). His lawsuit (option F) followed his rejection. The Supreme Court decision (option G) followed Bakke's lawsuit. [Sequence]

19. A The passage discusses the makeup of the student population in colleges, and students are a group of persons. Options B, C, and D are incorrect because they do not fit the topic of the passage. [Same Meaning]

20. G Option G is correct because a volunteer for Habitat for Humanity International would support the goal of eliminating poverty housing and homelessness, as stated in the passage. The other choices are incorrect because HFHI does not focus on pollution (option F), education (option H), or the appearance of neighborhoods (option J). [Apply Passage Element]

21. B The third sentence of the first paragraph describes one family's inadequate housing situation. Option A is not correct because homeless people do not have apartments. Option C is not correct because Habitat for Humanity builds new homes. Option D is not correct because well-maintained housing does not have crumbling walls and ceilings. [Style Techniques]

22. F People who apply for Habitat housing want to have a decent and affordable place to live. The passage does not imply that they are unemployed (option G). They are not lazy (option H), because to be involved in the Habitat program you have to agree to help to build your own house and other houses. They probably don't have a high standard of living (option J) if they're wanting decent and affordable housing. [Conclusion]

23. B Option B is correct because Habitat for Humanity is dedicated to building homes for low-income families. Therefore, a wealthy person would not qualify for the program. Options A, C, and D are not correct because you do not need to predict these things. The paragraph already clearly states them. [Apply Passage Element]

24. H Option H is correct because only a decreasing supply of affordable housing could help explain the housing problem, and *growing* means the opposite of *decreasing*. A large supply would not be a problem, so Option F (large) is incorrect. The *-ing* ending in *diminishing* implies a changing situation. Option G does not have this word ending and thus does not imply change, so it is incorrect. Option J is incorrect because *decreasing* means the same, not the opposite, of *diminishing*. [Opposite Meaning]

25. B Option B is correct because the passage covers basic points about Habitat for Humanity and does not assume the reader has any prior knowledge of the organization. Option A is incorrect because the main focus is on who benefits from Habitat for Humanity, not on volunteers. Option C is incorrect because the passage is supportive rather than critical of the organization. Option D is incorrect because homelessness is not the main topic. [Author's Purpose]

26. G Line 2 of the form states "I will be out of the country on election day," which is the case for Ms. Koso. Option F is incorrect because Ms. Koso is 29 years old. Option H is incorrect because Ms. Koso's religious beliefs are not related to her decision to apply for an absent voter's ballot. Option J is incorrect because she is not claiming that she is on active duty with the organized militia in the State of Ohio. [Forms]

27. D Item 10 in the list of reasons for being absent states that confinement in jail is an acceptable excuse only if the applicant is under sentence for a misdemeanor or "waiting trial on a felony or misdemeanor." The other options are incorrect because they are on the list as items 4, 3, and 1. [Forms]

28. H Option H is correct because the passage states that Ms. Koso wants to vote in the next general election for president. Options G and J are incorrect because Ms. Koso is not concerned about a special election (option G) or a primary election (option J). Option F is incorrect because "other party" relates to the choice of primary election. [Forms]

29. C Note 2 at the bottom of the form states that "an application by mail must be received by the Board of Elections by noon on the third day before the election." Option A is incorrect because this deadline applies only to persons who are hospitalized by a medical emergency (see note 2). Option B is incorrect because this deadline applies to sending in a completed ballot, not the application form (see note 3). Option D is incorrect because this deadline applies to applications by the voter in person (see note 2). [Detail]

30. J The Board of Elections is the organization responsible for overseeing absentee balloting, so option J is the correct answer. Option F is not correct because companies do not usually hand out political materials to employees. The post office (option G) and the Department of Motor Vehicles (option H) are not the most likely source of the form. [Conclusion]

31. D The passage states that during Operation Desert Storm Powell gave frequent press conferences to the nation. Option A is incorrect because Powell's service during the Vietnam War did not draw wide public attention. Option B is incorrect because Powell's cousin, not Powell, is a federal judge. Option C is incorrect because the passage does not mention Powell's autobiography. [Conclusion]

32. H The passage is about a notable African American. Option F is incorrect because only part of the passage is about the Gulf War. Options G and J are incorrect because the passage does not focus on military training (option G) or the inside workings of the White House (option J). [Genre]

33. D Powell has always aimed high and tried to be the best. The passage states that he is dedicated to helping youth live up to high expectations and achieve their dreams. The passage does not suggest that Powell always wanted to train soldiers (option A), or that he has always been concerned about racism (option B). Although Powell may have a deep understanding of energy and budget issues (option C), this cannot be determined from the information in the paragraph. [Apply Passage Element]

34. H America's Promise is a group that helps young people succeed by creating high expectations, and the passage implies that Powell's parents had high expectations of him. Options F and G are incorrect because they relate to the military, not helping youth. Option J is incorrect because the fellowship relates to political service, not youth. [Cause and Effect]

35. A Powell took on several high-ranking political positions. Option B is incorrect because his service in the military and national government shows his sense of duty to his country. Option C is incorrect because his founding of America's Promise shows his commitment to youth. Option D is incorrect because he did serve courageously in Vietnam. [Supporting Evidence]

36. J Powell is an African American and a general, and the passage focuses on his leadership. Options F and H are incorrect because they describe only parts of the passage and Powell's life. Option G is incorrect because the passage does not say that Powell was disadvantaged or that he ever encountered great obstacles. [Summary and Paraphrase]

37. D Option D is correct because it states something about Powell that can be proved: Powell joined the ROTC to train as a military officer while in college. Options A, B, and C are incorrect because they use words that make a judgment: "excellent" (option A), "best" (option B), and "most admired" (option C). [Fact and Opinion]

38. F Paragraph 5 of the passage describes the *chassis* as something "flat" that the top of the car fits onto. This description fits the meaning "frame," or structure. It does not fit the idea of wheels (option G), an engine (option H), or a cockpit (option J); so these choices are incorrect. [Same Meaning]

39. A According to the passage, electronic controls take up almost no space and replace parts such as the brake pedal, steering wheel, and throttle. Options B and D are incorrect because they do not accurately describe hydrogen cars. Option C is incorrect because producing water does not affect the roominess of the car. [Stated Concept]

40. H The paragraph discusses the need for a new infrastructure—plants and distribution equipment—to support the production of hydrogen cars, which will take a long time to build. Option F is incorrect because hydrogen cars are not yet popular. Options G and J are incorrect because they are supporting details in the paragraph, not the main point. [Main Idea]

41. C Paragraph 3 explains that the fuel cell splits hydrogen atoms, releasing electrons that power the car. Options A, B, and D are untrue statements and thus are incorrect. [Conclusion]

42. G The passage discusses benefits of hydrogen cars, such as their "environmental friendliness" and roominess. Option F is incorrect because the passage does not summarize any research. Options H and J are incorrect because they do not reflect the main focus of the passage. [Author Purpose]

43. C This option is correct because water and heat are not harmful byproducts compared to those produced by ICE cars, such as carbon monoxide. Options A, B, and D are incorrect because they do not focus on environmental effects. [Supporting Evidence]

44. H This choice is supported by information in paragraph 3. The other choices do not reflect the facts, as stated in the passage. [Supporting Evidence]

45. D Option D is correct because "the peoples of early North America" is the subtitle of the book. It appears in the second line of the card after the colon and clarifies the title *Red, White and Black*. Option A is incorrect because the publication date is 1992. This date appears after the publisher's name in line 3 of the card. Option B is incorrect because 340 refers to the number of pages, not illustrations. Option C is incorrect because it refers to one of the subjects of the book, which are listed at the bottom of the card. [Library Catalog Card Display]

46. J Option J is correct because it appears as the first subject in the numerical listing of subjects at the bottom of the card. The first topic represents the book's main topic and is used to classify the book. Option F is incorrect because nonfiction books are not classified by author. Option G is incorrect because Dewey classifications are based on a book's content, not whether it has maps or illustrations. Option H is incorrect because "American history" is a very broad subject, while this book focuses on a specific period. [Library Catalog Card Display]

47. D Option D is correct because this card is for the subject "America—Discovery and Exploration," as shown by the heading at the top of the card. Option C is where a card for the author would be filed. Option A is where the card for the book's title would be filed. Option B is where the card for the other subjects, beginning with "United States," would be filed. [Library Catalog Card Display]

48. G Option G is the most specific topic. Options F, H, and J are vast topics that include many different types of information. [Reference Sources]

49. B Option B is correct because an atlas is a collection of maps. Options A and D are incorrect because these are references for words. Option C is incorrect because an almanac is a compact collection of facts and statistics. [Reference Sources]

50. G Most libraries shelve all of their nonfiction books by call number, making options F, H, and J incorrect. [Reference Sources]

Performance Assessment: Language (pages 49–61)

A. D Option D has correct grammar, punctuation, and spelling. In option A, *I* should be *me*. In option B, *brought* should be future tense *will bring*. Option C is a fragment.

B. J Option J has correct capitalization and punctuation. Option F is a run-on sentence. Option G should not end with a question mark. Option H should end with a question mark.

C. B Option B communicates the cause and effect relationship between Max's buying habits and the stuffed state of his closet. In options A, C, and D, the meaning of the sentences is altered.

D. H Option H corrects the run-on sentence by punctuating the first one with a question mark and starting the second one with a capital letter. Option F is not correct because the second sentence begins with a lowercase letter. Option G is not correct because the first sentence, a question, ends with a period. Option J is not correct because the first sentence is a question and should end with a question mark, not an exclamation point.

1. D The sentence is correct as written and punctuated. It is not a question (option A). It does not need an additional comma (option B) or a period (option C). [Commas]

2. H Option H is correct because the question should end with a question mark after *connection*. It does not need a comma (option F) or an additional period (option G). Option J is not correct because the question needs a question mark. [Question Marks]

3. A Because Brittney is yelling, an exclamation point is needed inside the first closing quotation mark. When a quotation is divided into two parts by an

expression, such as *Brittany yelled*, the first part should end with a comma. However, "Watch out!" is a complete statement, so it does not need a comma (option B) or a period (option C), but it does need an end mark (option D). [Quotation Marks]

4. G In option G, *bring* is used correctly to indicate something that moves toward someone or something. In options F, H, and J the meaning of *bring* and *take* are confused. [Easily Confused Verbs]

5. C Option C uses quotation marks correctly. Option A is not correct because it does not include a quotation, but it has quotation marks. Option B should have closing quotation marks after *Well*. Option D should have opening quotation marks before *Either*. [Quotation Marks]

6. J The modifiers in option J are correctly placed. In option F, *from the Chinese market* incorrectly modifies *sack*. In option G *often* should precede *healthier*. In option H, *bite-size* incorrectly modifies *vegetables* when it should modify *pieces*. [Misplaced Modifier]

7. C Option C is correct because the subject and verb agree in number. In options A and D, *are* should be *is*. In option B, *eats* should be *eat*. [Subject and Verb Agreement]

8. H In option H, *park* and *use* have parallel structure. In option F, *if you take* should be *taking*. In option G, *they have the* should be deleted. In option J, *you have to bend* should be *bending*. [Nonparallel Structure]

9. D In option D, the proper nouns are capitalized. In option A, *dollhouse* should be capitalized. In option B, *tuesday* should be capitalized. In option C, *Bar Exams* should not capitalized. [Capitalization]

10. F In option F, the pronoun agrees with its antecedent. In option G, *he* should be *she*. In option H, *they* should be *she*. In option J, *her* should be *their*. [Antecedent Agreement]

11. A Option A is properly capitalized. In option B, *Book Critics'* should not be capitalized. In option C, *december* and *everlasting* should be capitalized. In option D, *Novel* should not. [Capitalization]

12. H In option H, the semicolon is used to separate two closely related sentences. In options F and G, the colon should be a semicolon. The first sentence in option J should end with a period, not with a semicolon, because the two sentences are not closely related. [Semicolon]

13. D In option D, the geographic term and the month of the year are capitalized. In option A, *Internist* should not be capitalized; in option B, *hospital* should be capitalized; and in option C, *hospital* and *grand* should be capitalized. [Capitalization]

14. J In option J, the subject and verb agree and the tense is correct. In the other choices, either the subject and verb do not agree or the tenses in the clauses do not agree. [Subject and Verb Agreement]

15. C Option C is a superlative adverb, which is required in the sentence. Options A and B are incorrectly formed comparative and superlative adverbs.

Option D is not correct because it is the adverb form used to compare just two things. [Adverb]

16. J Option J is correct because it is in the past progressive tense, which is required because in the sentence a past action is interrupted by another past action. Option F is not correct because it is in the present tense. Option G is not correct because it is in the past tense. Option H is not correct because it is in the present progressive tense. [Progressive Tense]

17. D Option D is unrelated to the main idea of the paragraph, which is the sighting of coyotes in urban areas. The other options are related to the main idea of the paragraph. [Unrelated Sentence]

18. H Option H is unrelated to the topic of the paragraph, which is wooden roller coasters. Options F, G, and J are all related to the topic of the paragraph. [Unrelated Sentence]

19. D Option D gives an additional detail, or supports, the topic sentence. Options A, B, and C do not support the topic sentence. [Supporting Sentences]

20. G Option G gives additional detail, or supports, the topic sentence. Options F, H, and J do not support the topic sentence. [Supporting Sentences]

21. A Option A best combines and maintains the meaning of the two sentences. In options B, C, and D, the meaning of the sentences has been altered. [Coordinating]

22. G In option G, the two sentences are correctly combined using *while* to show contrast. In options F, H, and J, the meaning of the sentences has been altered. [Adding Modifier]

23. D In option D, the subordinating sentence is combined with the main sentence in a way that preserves the meaning of both sentences. In options A, B, and C, the meaning of the sentences has been altered. [Subordinating]

24. H Option H is the only sentence that combines the coordinating sentences in a way that preserves the meaning of both sentences. In options F, G, and J, the meaning of the sentences has been altered. [Coordinating]

25. D Option D fits into the proper sequence in the paragraph. Option A would fit well following the current first sentence, but it would be out of sequence as the third sentence. Option B would make a good final sentence, but would be out of sequence as the third sentence. Option C would make a good new first sentence, but would be out of sequence as the third sentence. [Sequence]

26. F Option F is the topic sentence on which the other sentences in the paragraph expand. Options G, H, and J are too specific and detailed to be topic sentences. [Topic Sentence]

27. C Option C includes the transition word *therefore* and correctly draws a conclusion from all the information in the paragraph. The sentences and transition words in options A, B, and D do not draw a conclusion. [Connective and Transition]

28. H Option H is the topic sentence on which the rest of the paragraph is based. Options F, G, and J are too specific and detailed to be a topic sentences. [Topic Sentence]

29. A In option A, the transition word *however* indicates the proper relationship of the information in the sentence to the rest of the paragraph. In option B, *Therefore* confuses the meaning because it indicates a cause-and-effect relationship where there is none. In option C, *Likewise* indicates a comparison where there is none. Option D does not make sense because a specific *tradition* is not discussed in the paragraph. [Connective and Transition]

30. J Option J makes sense as a concluding sentence. Options F, G, and H describe details that are too early in the sequence of events to be used as a concluding sentence. [Sequence]

31. C Option C is the only answer choice that uses a comma correctly after the date. Option A lacks a comma, option B has a misplaced comma, and option D has an extraneous comma. [Parts of a Letter]

32. F Option F is correct because a comma is not necessary in this part of the address. Options G and J each have one extraneous comma, and option H has two extraneous commas. [Parts of a Letter]

33. C In option C, the salutation is correctly punctuated with a colon. In option A, the semicolon should be a colon. In option B, *ms.* should be capitalized. In option D, there should be a colon after *Pinella*. [Parts of a Letter]

34. H In option H, negative words are used correctly. The other choices have double negatives. Options F and J have *not* and *never*; option G has *don't* and *never*. [Use Negative]

35. C In option C, the parenthetical expression is correctly set off by commas. In option A, there are two commas missing. In options B and D, there is one comma missing. [Commas]

36. H Option H divides and punctuates the run-on into two sentences. Option F, G, and J are run-on sentences. [Sentence Recognition]

37. B In option B, the closing is capitalized correctly and punctuated with a comma. In option A, *very* should be capitalized and *yours* should be followed by a comma. In option C, *Truly* should not be capitalized. In option D, *very* should be capitalized. [Parts of a Letter]

38. G In option G, the appositive is set off from the rest of the sentence with commas. In option F, the colon should be a comma. In option H, the semicolon should be a comma. In option J, there should be a comma following *Michigan*. [Commas]

39. A In option A, negatives are used correctly and the writer's intent is maintained. In options B and C, the meaning is altered. In option D, there are two negatives, *no* and *nowhere*. [Use Negative]

40. F The sentence requires an adjective to modify a noun. Option F is the only option that contains a correctly formed adjective. [Choose Between Adjective and Adverb]

41. D In option D, two closely related sentences are separated with a semicolon. Options A, B, and C use incorrect punctuation. [Semicolon]

42. F Option F is correct because the pronoun *it* agrees in number and meaning with the antecedent *Grand Haven*. [Antecedent Agreement]

43. B Option B is an adjective that has parallel structure with the other two adjectives in the sentence. Options A, C, and D do not have parallel structure with the other two adjectives in the sentence. [Nonparallel Structure]

44. G Option G uses negatives correctly. Options F and H have altered meanings, and option J has two negatives, *no* and *doesn't*. [Use Negative]

45. B The sentence requires an adjective to modify the noun *bodies*. Option B is the correct adjective form of *muscle*. Options A, C, and D are incorrectly formed. [Choose Between Adjective and Adverb]

46. J Option J is correct because it is in the future tense. Option F is incorrect because it is awkward and not in the correct tense. Option G is not correct because it is singular. Option H is not correct because it is in the past tense. [Future Tense]

47. B Option B is capitalized correctly. In option A, *In* should not be capitalized. In option C, *dancing* and *starlight* should be capitalized. In option D, *starlight* should be capitalized. [Capitalization]

48. H Option H is capitalized correctly. In options F, G, and J, the name of the film festival is incorrectly capitalized. [Capitalization]

49. A Option A is correct because an adjective is needed to modify the noun *competition*. Options B and C incorrectly make a comparison. Option D is an adverb. [Choose Between Adjective and Adverb]

50. H In option H, the parenthetical expression *Gosh* is properly separated from the rest of the sentence. In option F, the period should be a comma. In option G, the colon should be a comma. In option J, there should be a comma after *Gosh*. [Commas]

51. A Option A is the least verbose option. Options B, C, and D each use two essentially similar words when only one is needed. [Verbosity and Repetition]

52. F Option F is in the correct possessive form. Options G and H have misplaced apostrophes, and option J lacks an apostrophe. [Apostrophe]

53. D In option D, the modifying phrase is placed correctly. Options A, B, and C all include misplaced modifiers. [Misplaced Modifier]

54. F Option F corrects the sentence. Options G, H, and J include unnecessary punctuation. [Punctuation]

55. D The sentence is correct as it is because the plural pronoun *their* agrees with the plural noun *companies*. Option B is not correct because it is singular. Options A and C are singular and gender-specific, while the antecedent is plural and gender-neutral. [Antecedent Agreement]

A. C Option C is spelled correctly and has the correct meaning. Option A is a homonym of *weather* and has a different meaning. Option B is misspelled and option D is a different word.

1. C In option C, the root is spelled correctly. Options A, B, and D are misspelled. [Root]

2. F *Impartial* is the correct spelling. The *sh* sound is spelled with a *ti*. Options G, H, and J are misspelled. [Variant Spelling Consonants]

3. C In option C, the suffix *–ance* is spelled correctly. Options A, B, and D are misspelled. [Similar Word Part]

4. J In option J, the short vowel is spelled correctly. Options F, G, and H are misspelled. [Short Vowel]

5. B In option B, both double consonants are spelled correctly. Options A, C, and D are misspelled. [Double Letter Consonants]

6. J In option J, the silent letters are spelled correctly. Options F, G, and H are misspelled. [Silent Letter Consonants]

7. A In option A, the schwa sound is spelled correctly with an *i*. Options B, C, and D are misspelled. [Schwa]

8. H In option H, the *s* sound is spelled correctly with a *c*. Options F, G, and J are misspelled. [Variant Spelling Consonants]

9. D In option D, the suffix *–ous* is spelled correctly. Options A, B, and C are misspelled. [Suffix]

10. H In option H, the *s* sound is spelled correctly with a *c*. Options F, G, and J are misspelled. [Variant Spelling Consonants]

11. C In option C, the short vowel sound is spelled correctly. Options A, B, and D are misspelled. [Short Vowel]

12. J In option J, the schwa sound is spelled with the correct vowel. Options F, G, and H are misspelled. [Schwa]

13. A In option A, the word part *–ent* is spelled correctly. Options B, C, and D are misspelled. [Similar Word Part]

14. H In option H, the suffix is spelled correctly. Options F, G, and J are misspelled. [Suffix]

15. C In option C, the ending schwa sound is spelled correctly. Options A, B, and D are misspelled. [Schwa]

16. G In option G, the *s* sound is spelled correctly with a *c*. Options F, H, and J are misspelled. [Consonant]

17. C In option C, the long *e* sound is spelled correctly. Options A, B, and D are misspelled. [Long Vowel]

18. J In option J, the double consonant is spelled correctly. Options F, G, and H are misspelled. [Consonants]

19. C In option C, the schwa sound is spelled correctly with *u*. Options A, B, and D are misspelled. [Schwa]

20. F In option F, the word part *–ant* is spelled correctly. Options G, H, and J are misspelled. [Similar Word Part]